W9-CBT-415

I love working with John, and *Beyond Boundaries* is a must for everyone who read *Boundaries*. This is his best book yet.

—STEPHEN ARTERBURN, Bestselling Author,
Host of *New Life Live!* radio talk show

Beyond Boundaries is the perfect compass for navigating the rough waters of challenging relationships. Everyone will benefit from Dr. Townsend's wisdom on living on the healthy side of life.

—CRAIG GROESCHEL, Senior Pastor of LifeChurch.tv,
Author of *Weird: Because Normal Isn't Working*

We're all sinners, and as a result we have the capacity to hurt—and to be hurt—in all of our relationships. Thankfully, for those willing to do the work, Dr. John Townsend's book provides a roadmap back to healing, trust, and restoration.

—JIM DALY, President, Focus on the Family

In *Beyond Boundaries*, John Townsend gives us the long-awaited next step to his and Henry Cloud's book *Boundaries*! Marriages will be made stronger and all of our important relationships will be more intimate and authentic! I highly recommend this book for everyone. It is a must read!

—JOHN BAKER, Pastor and Founder
of Celebrate Recovery

This is one of the best books I have ever read on building healthy relationships. I marked up almost every page. John Townsend is one America's finest communicators on this subject. I read everything John writes and am a better person for it.

—JIM BURNS, PhD, President, HomeWord,
Author of *Creating an Intimate Marriage and Closer:
Devotions to Draw Couples Together*

BEYOND BOUNDARIES

LEARNING TO TRUST AGAIN IN RELATIONSHIPS

DR. JOHN TOWNSEND

foreword by DR. HENRY CLOUD, coauthor of *Boundaries*

ZONDERVAN.com/
AUTHORTRACKER
follow your favorite authors

We want to hear from you. Please send your comments about this book to us in care of zreview@zondervan.com. Thank you.

ZONDERVAN

Beyond Boundaries
Copyright © 2011 by Dr. John Townsend

This title is also available as a Zondervan ebook. Visit www.zondervan.com/ebooks.

This title is also available in a Zondervan audio edition. Visit www.zondervan.fm.

Requests for information should be addressed to:

Zondervan, *Grand Rapids, Michigan 49530*

Library of Congress Cataloging-in-Publication Data

Townsend, John Sims, 1952 –
    Beyond boundaries : learning to trust again in relationships / Dr. John Townsend.
       p.   cm.
    Includes bibliographical references.
    ISBN 978-0-310-33049-3 (hardcover, jacketed)
    1. Intimacy (Psychology) – Religious aspects – Christianity. 2. Loss (Psychology)
– Religious aspects – Christianity. 3. Risk-taking (Psychology) – Religious aspects
– Christianity. I. Title.
    BV4597.53.I55T69 2011
    158.2 – dc22   2011015881

All Scripture quotations, unless otherwise indicated, are taken from the Holy Bible, *New International Version®, NIV®.* Copyright © 1973, 1978, 1984, 2011 by Biblica, Inc.™ Used by permission of Zondervan. All rights reserved worldwide.

Any Internet addresses (websites, blogs, etc.) and telephone numbers printed in this book are offered as a resource. They are not intended in any way to be or imply an endorsement by Zondervan, nor does Zondervan vouch for the content of these sites and numbers for the life of this book.

All rights reserved. No part of this publication may be reproduced, stored in a retrieval system, or transmitted in any form or by any means — electronic, mechanical, photocopy, recording, or any other — except for brief quotations in printed reviews, without the prior permission of the publisher.

Published in association with Yates & Yates, www.yates2.com.

Cover design: Extra Credit Projects
Cover photography: GettyImages®
Interior design: Beth Shagene

Printed in the United States of America

---

11 12 13 14 15 16 17 /DCI/ 22 21 20 19 18 17 16 15 14 13 12 11 10 9 8 7 6 5 4 3

*To all who believe that relationships
are worth the risk. God bless you.*

Acknowledgments

To Sealy Yates, my literary agent: for your commitment to quality books and your tireless work in making a context for them to be crafted.

To Moe Girkins, former CEO of Zondervan Publishing: for your vision and support for this book's concept and value.

To Sandy Vander Zicht, executive editor, Zondervan Publishing: for your creativity in working with the original idea and your dedication to the process.

To Greg Campbell: for your strategic design and the time you spent responding to the content.

To my wife, Barbi: for your love, support, and thoughtful responses during the writing period.

To the members of my Leadership Coaching Program teams: for your dedication to personal and professional growth and for sharing your own stories of moving beyond boundaries.

Contents

Foreword

I remember the day John and I decided to write *Boundaries* as though it were yesterday. We were in a planning meeting, and someone asked, "When the two of you speak, what topic do you get the most questions about?" We both burst out laughing and said, "Boundaries." All of the questions were about boundaries.

So, the next question he posed was, "So why don't you write a book about your system of boundaries?" Immediately John and I looked at each other and thought: "That's a great idea! If we wrote a book on boundaries, it would answer all those questions, and we would be able to stop talking about boundaries and go on to the other topics we needed to address."

Little did we know that the *opposite* would happen. We had no idea how big the need was to continue talking about boundaries. The lack of boundaries is such a human problem, and the pain caused by boundary violations is so great, that we will be talking about boundaries until the day we die. Virtually everyone needs to understand boundaries and how setting them is essential to experiencing freedom in every area of life. Where boundaries fail, relationships fail, people hurt, and life performance suffers. Boundaries affect us psychologically, relationally, physically, and spiritually.

Now, fast forward to today, where we find ourselves in a similar moment. If you asked us, "After people have worked on their boundaries and have stopped the destruction and the pain, what's next? What's beyond boundaries?" We would have to say, "Well, after the pain is over, it's time to trust again, and this time be much smarter about it. It's time to rebuild relationships, and your life, and have good boundaries in place that will keep you safe and ensure the life you desire. This is what 'beyond boundaries' is." John has written a book to be your guide to trusting again, so this time you can do it better.

Whether it means trusting in a relationship where trust has been broken, or establishing new relationships with good boundaries, or just defining your future in a healthy way, this book will help you. I can attest to that for two reasons.

First, John is an obvious expert on the topic. For over twenty years he has taught boundaries to millions of people on the radio, in live seminars, and in various work and consulting situations. There is not a boundary question he hasn't heard and can't answer. So, you can trust his expertise. This is not academic theory from him, but real answers that have been tested and proven over time in the real world.

Second, John is a trustworthy character, whom I have seen practice and live out what he preaches in the decades we have worked together. In his personal life and his professional life, you will not find a situation where he is out of sync with his message. To me, this is as important as his expertise. He is not trying to get you to do something he does not do himself. This is why I have trusted him implicitly as a business partner and a close friend since graduate school. I think you can to.

Now that you have good boundaries and are ready to take the next step, let this book be your guide to becoming the person you were created to be, having good relationships with the right people, and getting closer to the God who created it all.

HENRY CLOUD, Ph.D., Los Angeles, 2011

Don't Settle

If you don't want to settle in your relational life, this book is for you.

Settling or adapting to less than you're capable of is often necessary in other aspects of our lives. Golf pros have to settle for playing the senior tour at some point. Individuals and families have to settle for spending less and adjusting their financial budgets to fit their circumstances. Parents eventually have to settle for releasing control of their children and allowing them to make their own choices. But in the world of relationships, we often settle far too soon.

When we experience a difficult and uncomfortable relationship — in marriage, dating, family, friendship, or work — we have a tendency to withdraw. That is natural and often necessary. Pain creates a withdrawal response to protect us from further discomfort or damage. When I was a teenager and started shaving, I used to nick my face with the razor. I hated that sharp slicing pain, and I would quickly pull the razor away and finish the job, staying away from that area of my face. I didn't look forward to my next shaving session and wanted to avoid it. But in time, I learned how to keep the razor at the right angle and to use a smooth stroke.

People settle in different ways, adapting to what they think is the best possible scenario. Some settle by staying in a pleasantly tolerable marriage — not adversarial, but not close. Some by dating a succession of people without ever making a commitment. Some by keeping even their most important friendships at a comfortable distance. And some by redirecting their energies and focus into activities rather than relationships.

Settling in relationships isn't the worst way to go through life. It's fairly painless and often predictable. There is some value in pain avoidance and predictability, but it is far from how you are designed to live. More than anything in the world, you are meant to connect and relate in deep, meaningful, and positive relationships—with both God and people. This is the means and the end of a good and happy life.

The challenge comes when our closest relationships become unhealthy or even toxic. At such times it's essential to establish healthy relational boundaries to protect ourselves. When Henry Cloud and I wrote about this issue two decades ago in our book *Boundaries*,[1] we had no idea how much interest people would have in the book, nor in the succeeding books on marriage, dating, parenting, teens, and having difficult conversations. But in conferences, radio interactions, emails, social network connections, and one-on-one conversations, we discovered that many Christians had no understanding of what the Bible teaches about personal responsibility, especially where it ends and where it begins. Although they had learned a great deal about giving, caring, loving, sacrificing, and forgiving, they had little understanding about other significant issues—what they should and should not take ownership of in a relationship, what choices to fight for, and how not to enable toxic patterns such as addictions, sin, and abuse. We were happy to see so many people finally learning to say no when they needed to and finding the freedom of choice that God promises us: "It is for freedom that Christ set us free; Stand firm, therefore, and do let yourselves be burdened again by a yoke of slavery" (Galatians 5:1). People were learning to make their own decisions, based on their own values, and were finding a great deal of happiness and fulfillment.

But over the years, a significant question emerged: *Once I have had a relational problem and have had to set a limit, how do I know when to take a risk again with someone?* This is a question driven by a desire for connectedness and relationship, which God embedded in every human being. By definition, learning to set appropriate limits causes a degree of separation between you and another person. It may mean staying within the relationship and not allowing someone else access to your deeper self. It may mean taking a timeout from the relationship. Or it may even mean ending the connection altogether, depending on the circumstances. Whatever the situation, people found that though they were happy with the freedom their boundaries provided, they still wanted connectedness and often didn't know how to reestablish it—in their existing relationship or a new one.

That is why this book is called *Beyond Boundaries.* It is designed to teach you how to identify and grow from whatever went wrong in the relationship, help you to determine if someone is worthy of your trust now, and show you how to manage the process of opening up in a gradual and safe way. Once you have set your boundaries, when the time is right, you can go beyond the boundaries that have kept you protected and on the other side to also find great relationships, depth, and freedom in your connections, which is the place where God meant you to be all along.

A Vision of Life *Beyond Boundaries*

Here are a few examples of how I have seen people move beyond boundaries:

In the workplace. Glenn and Rich, both friends of mine, were partners in an investment firm. Things got difficult between them, and the situation didn't draw out the best in the two. They blamed each other, lost trust, and eventually dissolved the partnership. I was saddened by this, not only because I liked both men, but also because I knew they were a great team. However, their self-imposed boundaries with each other gave them both time to reflect and grow. They practiced the principles in this book, and within a few years they were collaborating on a project together again.

In marriage. Teresa and Keith were in a twelve-year marriage that was a train wreck. Keith was verbally harsh and self-centered; Teresa was needy and afraid of conflict. When I started seeing them as a couple, it was clear that though they cared about each other and the marriage, they were alienated and felt hopeless about the future.

In the course of the counseling, Teresa had to set clear boundaries with Keith. When he became harsh and critical, Teresa usually complied and gave in just to keep the peace and at least have some connection with him. But she learned to tell him clearly,"I care about us, but this behavior hurts me and isn't acceptable. If you won't be kinder to me, I'll go to another room and may even ask you to leave the house until you choose to stop this." And Teresa had to do that for a while.

Gradually, Keith began to change inside. He softened up and connected to Teresa. Uncertain if the change was authentic, she did not immediately become vulnerable with him. But over time they developed a real closeness with each other and today are a seasoned and intimate couple who enjoy their life together.

In families. Lindsay's mom drove her crazy. Though Lindsay was married and a mother herself, her mom persisted in trying to control and mother Lindsay. When she visited Lindsay's home, her mom critiqued her parenting. Lindsay would spend hours with her mom, who was lonely and had few friends, only to hear her mom tell Lindsay she wasn't with her enough.

Finally, Lindsay had to set a boundary. She told her mom they couldn't see each other as much. Lindsay needed some time to develop better ways to cope with her mom on a healthier level. And though her mom never really understood why this was so, Lindsay was eventually able to reenter the relationship with more energy, clarity, and even love for her mom.

In my own life. When I was in my grad school years, I had a friend, Dan, whom I didn't really treat as a good friend. I spent time with him when I felt like it, but when it was inconvenient, I was unavailable. I would find some excuse for going out to dinner or on a double date with our girlfriends. I'm not proud of this, but it is a reality, and I think I am a different person now. Anyway, it took a while and a lot of distance between us, but Dan and I became friends again, and the relationship is much more mutual and balanced than it was before.

My prayer is that the stories, insights, and skills presented in *Beyond Boundaries* will help you to move beyond your own withdrawals and settle back into taking some relational risks, the purpose of which is intimacy. Although there are real risks and there will always be the possibility of hurt, it is possible to make the risks manageable, reasonable, and doable. You may have to settle, however, for less than the other person is willing and able to do. But if you do settle, the limiting factor won't be you.

Redeeming Losses

Jerry and Val Reddix are career missionaries and longtime friends of Barbi and me. Jerry and I went through our doctoral programs in psychology together. During that time, Val became pregnant with their third child. One day, Barbi and I got a call saying they were at the hospital because something had gone wrong with the baby. When we arrived, Jerry told us that Michael had been born, but he had life-threatening issues and was not expected to survive very long, maybe a matter of weeks. He would be staying at the hospital for whatever help he could receive. Our hearts were broken. We really had no words for what Jerry and Val were going through. We were just deeply and terribly sad for them.

We stayed in touch with Jerry and Val and visited when we could. Michael had good days and bad days. One morning, the Reddixes called us within a few minutes of Michael's death to tell us the news. We rushed to the hospital. The nurse brought Michael in, and they let us hold him for a few minutes, in both a hello and a good-bye. Then the nurse took him away. In that moment we entered the grief process with Jerry and Val. Barbi and I spent as much time simply being with them as we could, listening and being present. They talked about their own dreams for Michael and what it felt like to be so attached to him.

After Michael's passing, we stayed in touch, but then Jerry and Val moved away. A couple of years after their move, we heard that they had had another son whom they named Isaac. Since we were living in different parts of the country, we didn't see each other much. A number of years later, they, their two daughters, and Isaac visited us at our home. Isaac was about six years old. During the visit, I saw Jerry take Isaac aside and tell him, "You see these people? They know Michael. They met him. If you ever have any questions about your brother, ask them, and they can talk to you."

It's been many years since that day. Isaac hasn't had to call us, but Jerry did something very important. He kept his son alive in the memories of his family. He connected his loss to his family and to us. He did not want to hide the memory, though painful, from his relationships. He did not want to ignore Michael to avoid vulnerability.

The same idea applies to you. You may not have lost a child, but you have lost something. Perhaps it was a relationship that you hoped would last a lifetime, or your ability to trust and be open. Whatever your loss or whatever your hurt, you are designed to live in relationship, to reconnect, and to be vulnerable. Your difficulties can be redeemed and your self-protection resolved, if you move into the right paths.

Intimacy is complex, but it's not mysterious. Just as the laws of boundaries are clear, so are the rules of closeness and risk. You were meant to live beyond self-protection and to become close to other people again. It is well worth the risks and the effort to have the relationships you truly desire.

PART 1

UNDERSTANDING THE PROBLEM

I recently spent a fun evening with a group of friends. Among them were Colleen and Ryan, a couple I have known for some time. They have a long-term marriage, close to thirty years. As we caught up with each other, I couldn't help but notice the energy between them. It came out in how they played different parts in the conversation ("I'll set the stage, but you describe the bizarre encounter with the neighbor"), how they told jokes on each other ("So he ignores the GPS and we lose an hour driving in circles"), how they supported each other ("Tell them how you're the first woman to get promoted in that department"), and how they looked at each other. It was a little as if those of us with them were part of their relationship, but also outside it as well. They had their own private club, though they were still connected to the rest of us.

If that encounter were the only information you had about

Ryan and Colleen, you might be tempted to hold them up as a model of intimacy and connectedness — a couple that somehow managed to avoid all the pitfalls that typically cause a long-term marriage to grow stale, disconnected, or worse. However, what most of the others present that evening did not know was that several years ago, Ryan and Colleen had come close to ending their relationship. Ryan had an affair that devastated Colleen. At the time, neither Ryan nor Colleen was sure whether they wanted to stay in the marriage. Had everyone present that evening been aware of this couple's history, they might have thought one of two things: that the two were faking things or that something miraculous had happened.

The latter was true. Colleen and Ryan experienced a miracle. Though it was far from instantaneous and involved a great deal of hard work, they went against the law of averages — as well as the expectations of the people who knew them — and reclaimed their relationship. They have become a new and different couple, relating on a much deeper level. Ryan has resolved the personal issues leading to the affair and is deeply in love with his wife. Colleen once again trusts her husband and has regained the love she once had for him.

I mention the story of Ryan and Colleen because it is a true story and one I hope will give you hope. If you're reading this book, I think it's safe to say that you probably have been burnt in a relationship that meant something to you. You may still be in the relationship and struggling to repair the damage. Or you may have moved on and don't want the past to repeat itself in a new connection. Either way, I started with Colleen and

Ryan's story because infidelity is one of the worst possible trust-breakers in a relationship. If this couple can make it, then perhaps you might be able to believe there is hope for your situation as well. We can learn to trust again, no matter what has happened, if we take the right path, step by step. And that is what this book is about.

In part 1, we look at how trust is broken in relationships in the first place, what happens to the person who is on the receiving end, and what happens to the relational connection. We explore the role that healthy boundaries play in protecting and healing people from further damage. We consider what happens when we begin experiencing the need and desire to find a new relationship or to try again with a present one, yet struggle with bad memories that keep us from being fully involved and engaged. All of this sets the stage for the three remaining parts: how to know when you are ready; how to know when the other person is ready; and how to begin the process of taking risks toward intimacy.

As you begin this path, it might help to remember that God is no stranger to the process of repairing damaged relationships. His trust has been broken many times by those he loves. Yet, he continues to take risks and experience the pain of reaching out when things aren't going well. God's own principles for restoring relationships provide the truth and guidance you need to help you get past your pain and to reexperience the intimacy you were designed for.

1

The Draw to Relationship

You and I are "drawn" to seek out relationships with others. We have an internal drive that propels us toward others. In fact, we have lots of other drives as well: we go online when we are information-driven. We walk to the kitchen when we are hunger-driven. We go shopping when we are clothing-driven. And we talk to people when we are relationship-driven. This isn't really an option. We are simply designed this way by God.

Our draw to relationship can be for companionship, business, love, or romance. The draw is strong and compelling. But it is not always well-informed, healthy, or full of good judgment. And so we often make bad choices, or we don't handle our relationships the way we should. We seek people out, not expecting to have to set boundaries. Then, after a relational struggle and some time in figuring out what happened, we again seek people out—we hope, in a wiser way. It is important to understand how completely drawn we are to finding others.

The problem of moving beyond boundaries begins by acknowledging a simple reality: we need to move beyond our self-protection because we are inevitably and permanently drawn to connect with others.

No one enters a relationship expecting a disaster. We don't anticipate things to run off the rails. We start off with hope, a desire for something good. We hope that friendship, intimacy, safety, and substance will develop. We hope that over time, the relationship will deepen and enrich our lives and perhaps lead to further commitment. This is where we want the relationship to go. In the beginning, we become interested in a person for many reasons: looks, shared interests, character, values, preferences. And once we determine that there might be potential for something good, we invest time and energy into seeing what can happen. But we always begin by hoping for the good.

This drive is not really a choice; it's an undeniable part of the way we're wired up. We are designed to seek out relationship and to hope that it will be a positive thing. We experience a "draw" — a move or a desire — to find someone outside of our own skin with whom we can share life. We want someone to understand us, to spend time with us, to help us find solutions to our problems. We are drawn outside of ourselves.

We find this in the first relationship in life, which is an infant's attachment to her mother. As soon as she emerges from the womb, she immediately searches for a presence to make her safe, protect her, and give her some semblance of predictability in the chaos of her first few minutes of life. It is an innate and instinctual act.

God created this draw toward relationship. The draw is toward himself, and we are told to look for his presence: "Seek the LORD while he may be found" (Isaiah 55:6). It is in relationship with God that we find ultimate connection and meaning. And by God's design, the draw is also toward others: "Two are better than one" (Ecclesiastes 4:9). We are at our best when we are connected deeply to God and to the people who matter most. That, along with a meaningful purpose and task, creates the best life possible.

Human connectedness provides a host of benefits for us. People who have healthy relationships live longer, have fewer health issues, and suffer fewer psychological disorders, to name a few areas. Relationships are simply the *fuel for life*, and they help power our activities and inner worlds in the directions they are to go. Isolation and destructive relationships, by contrast, are something to recover from, not something that benefits us.

Though most of us are aware of all the advantages of connection, we are not drawn to it primarily because of these benefits. We seek relationship because we want it and need it at a deep level that cannot be ignored. It can be pleasurable and fulfilling to love and be loved. And it can be painful and unfulfilling when things break down. We seek out jobs we feel passionate about, restaurants we love, and movies we feel alive in, all because we long for the experience of connection. The same is true for relationships.

The Trust Piece

For the draw to work as it should, however, any good relationship must have trust at its core. If you can trust the other person with your deeper self, the draw has done its job, and you can make a good connection. Most of us can handle relational problems, such as messiness, irresponsibility, or even high control. But when trust is not part of the equation, you simply don't know who is sitting in the chair across from you. It is the problem that must always be dealt with first. Trust is the ability to be vulnerable with another person. When you trust someone, you feel certain this person will keep your best interests in mind. You believe that they are who they say they are. You feel that the deepest parts of you will be safe with them. You expect that they will be there for you no matter what and that they will love you even when you are not so lovable.

Batach is one of the Hebrew words the Bible translates as *trust*. For example, "Commit your way to the LORD; *trust* in him and he will do this" (Psalm 37:5, emphasis added). One of the meanings of *batach* is "to be careless." It's not careless as in irresponsible or impulsive. It's care-*less*, as in without any cares or concerns. If you have a *batach* kind of trust, you feel free with someone; you don't have to edit yourself, be vigilant about what you say, or walk on eggshells. In *batach*, you open up a vulnerable part of yourself to God or another person without second-guessing or worrying about betrayal. That's trust.

Such trust is not a luxury, it is an essential.[2] Without trust, relationships cannot flourish. We all hope to find relationships in which we can rest in our trust that the other person is a safe person for us.

I once worked with a salesperson named Trevor. He had the perfect personality for sales: extroverted, energetic, and funny. But Trevor wasn't trustworthy. If he said he would be at a meeting at 10:00 a.m., he inevitably showed up at 10:20. If he called from his car and said he was ten minutes away, it was twenty. If he said he had made fifteen calls that day, the phone records indicated it was ten. It was difficult to work with him on this. In exasperation I finally said, "Trevor, I have to subtract 20 percent from everything you tell me in order to get an honest answer from you." In other words, though I wanted to trust him, I could not. My "draw" to him was diminished. Trust is the oil that keeps the relational machinery running smoothly. It is not a luxury. It is vital.

The Draw Isn't the Problem, We Are!

During my senior year in college, I encountered a double whammy: I had a girlfriend problem and a guy friend problem. The problems weren't related to each other, except that I was the common denominator. My girlfriend and I were at different places in our commitment to the relationship, so we were upside down. And my guy friend and I were at odds because we had a third friend who was in trouble with his conduct at school, and we were deeply divided over how to help him. One of us wanted to support him without any truth telling, and the other one didn't. You get the picture; I was in some relational messes.

At one point, I said to yet another friend, "I really hate this relational stuff. It would be a lot better just to have fun, and study, and work, and get out of all of this interpersonal trouble." In other words, I blamed the draw.

But the draw isn't the problem. You and I are the problem. Though it might seem easier to surgically remove your relational drive, you would lose the possibility of love, intimacy, joy, and meaning in life. It is something we all think about, however. You can't be deeply hurt or disappointed, withdraw from a connection, hesitate to get involved again, or, most important, struggle to trust again, unless your draw to relationship put you there in the first place. Had you not been relationship seeking and instead been a detached, disconnected, robotic person, you would not have encountered a relational problem.

Still, it's better to work on what is going on inside ourselves and deal with that than it is to disconnect, detach, and turn cold to relationships. To paraphrase Alfred Lord Tennyson's famous saying, rather than having loved and lost, you would have never loved at all. And it is always better to have some bruises than to never have tried to make a connection with someone. It is simply a central part of what makes life worth living.

Ultimately, the problem we run into is not our desire for relationship but how we respond to that desire. For example, our draw to relationship makes us vulnerable to self-deception. If you are with someone you care about, your hopes for the relationship can sometimes distort your perceptions. You might filter out information that doesn't fit the picture of what you're looking for and disregard it. This hope, which psychologists refer to as *defensive hope*, actually mismanages the experiences we have with people, distorting them toward a potentially unrealistic positive end.

For example, a man dating a woman who is possessive and demanding disregards her behavior by saying she is "more serious about the relationship" than he is. A mom with a teen who disrupts his classes at school calls him "spontaneous." A business owner with an office manager who won't take direction from him is "a strong-willed leader." We tend to polish the rotten apple because we want it to be a good apple.

Another aspect of this defensive hope is the "honeymoon period" in a relationship. Though "honeymoon" sounds like a new marriage, it refers to any new relationship period. It is the first few weeks of an important connection with someone, in which we see only the good: the other person's energy, talent, and personality. The honeymoon loads up our endorphins and keeps us in a positive state—for a while. Honeymoon periods are actually a form of "temporary psychosis." They provide a break from the reality of the negative and an exclusive acceptance of the positive. This is called an *idealization*, a perception that the other person is perfect or close to it.

These idealizing periods actually serve a good purpose. They help us store up good experiences in relationships so we have something to fall back on when we eventually wake up to reality: the first fight, failure, or performance problem. By the time the glitches occur, there is enough equity in the connection to deal with them, to solve the issues and reconnect with the other person.

In fact, specific marriage research now supports the idea that some form of idealization is a positive in ongoing relationships. Husbands and wives who see their partner in a more positive light than the spouse sees him or herself have more satisfying marriages.[3] For example, when one of them does something wrong, the other one first thinks that it was an innocent mistake. Of course, at some point, reality must set in, but this does show that, over time, a fundamentally positive bias about the person you love can help maintain your connection.

Perhaps you are regretting you ever trusted the person who caused your relational problem. If so, don't do that. You may have missed some warning signs, and we'll address those later so you won't miss them again. But understand that your draw to relationship is a part of you—a good and divine gift. You can mature it, educate it, and train it, but it doesn't go away. It is a healthy thing and an essential aspect of how God made you. Your best and highest situation is to be drawn to people, and to also have clarity on the character of who you're drawn to at the same time.

Now let's take a closer look at where the real trouble began —the thing that made it necessary for you to start setting boundaries and withdrawing from bad situations in the first place.

2

The Damage Arrives

I was working with Adam, an account executive for a large firm. He was a new hire and wanted to make a good first impression. His boss, Gene, was helpful and assisted Adam in settling in.

One day, Adam came up with some creative ideas about how the company could do a better job in sales. He told Gene about them, who seemed interested. A few days later, however, at a sales meeting, Adam heard Gene's boss compliment Gene on "coming up with some innovations that are a shot in the arm for the company." They were Adam's ideas.

Stunned, Adam met with Gene, who rationalized the entire situation. He told Adam that his recollection was that they had come up with the ideas together, and "I'll make sure you get credit with me." Adam could not get Gene to admit he had lied. And there was no recourse, as it was Gene's word against his.

Furthermore, Adam had to continue reporting to Gene. Adam tried hard to make it all work, but he was so discouraged and mistrustful of Gene that within a year he had to leave the company. He could not function at a high performance level, wondering all the time when Gene would again take credit for his ideas.

Adam encountered damage from Gene. Specifically, it was a *breach of trust in the relationship*. Everything stalled, because trust is foundational. It's important to be clear about what this means. A break in trust in relationship is when *you no longer experience or believe that the other person will always fundamentally be there for you, and you doubt that they are who they say they are.* When that happens, you have lost trust. It may not always be because of deception or lies. It can be because someone put herself first and didn't consider your interests at all — for example, when a friend uses you as the butt of her jokes at parties, even when you have asked her not to.

The Two Trusts

There are two types of trust in a relationship — functional trust and relational trust. In functional trust, you feel you can depend on the other person's behavior and commitments. For example, in a marriage, he'll pick up the clothes from the dry cleaner; she'll be home by 9:00 p.m. On a deeper level, she won't have inappropriate relationships with other men; he won't embezzle money from the retirement account. Functional trust has to do with the alignment between saying and doing: there is no discrepancy between words and actions. Functional trust is essential; it means you can be away from the other person and know there will be no surprises, ethical issues, or indiscretions in your absence. You don't have to monitor or check up on each other.

The second type of trust, relational trust, goes deeper. Relational trust refers to how safe it is to trust the other person with your vulnerabilities and feelings. For example, what does the other person do when you admit a weakness, reveal a need, admit a mistake, have a failure, or talk about trouble from your past? These are our more sensitive aspects and areas that need to be handled with care. When these issues manifest themselves in a relationship, the other person should understand that it was a huge risk for you to talk about them in the first place.

Here's what this might look like in a marriage. When a husband reveals a need or admits a mistake, his spouse should move toward him, be full of grace, and express tenderness and understanding. She can also be truthful and honest, but, keeping his vulnerability in mind, she needs to attempt to "restore [him] gently" (Galatians 6:1). If he cannot trust that she will at least try to understand, he will shut down emotionally. He thinks, *What is the use of being vulnerable? She won't even try to understand.*

Because it is deeper and more personal, a break in relational trust is a more serious problem than a break in functional trust. A financially irresponsible person—someone capable of breaking functional trust when it comes to money—may yet be trusted for how he feels toward you. You wouldn't want to trust him with your finances, but you can trust his concern for you in other areas. However, the reverse is not true. Someone who is responsible in areas related to functional trust but isn't safe with relational trust—responsive to your feelings and needs—is simply not someone you can safely get close to.

The damage comes when either functional or relational trust is broken. It can happen when the relationship undergoes stress: increased sales quotas, a new baby in the family, or a health problem. It can happen when there is conflict or failure: a job demotion, an argument over vacations or in-laws. And it can simply happen over time. Sooner or later, the passage of time unearths the flaws or weaknesses of the people in a relationship. These flaws cause a rupture in functional trust when someone lies, becomes irresponsible, or reveals a behavior or a secret that causes problems. Flaws and weaknesses cause a break in relational trust when the person becomes emotionally disconnected, controlling, critical, or self-absorbed.

When Trust Is Damaged

Trust—functional or relational—is the thread that holds two people together. When trust is damaged, the thread is severed and the disconnection begins. The person who has been hurt is often surprised, in shock, or in denial. She will often assume that she has misunderstood the situation or that it's her fault and she is responsible. She will feel guilty and take ownership of the problem. For example, when she is ignored emotionally, she may think, *I am asking too much from him and I'm pushing him away.* Although that may be true, she will act on it even if it's not true. She will do whatever it takes to restore the trust.

When you can no longer be assured that the other person is truly for you and relational trust is broken, several things happen that impact how you experience life. As you read the list the follows, see if you recognize any of these experiences in your own life. Going through this will help you make sense of why you are acting and feeling the way you are.

Withdrawal. You become careful instead of careless. You are more reserved about discussing personal information. You avoid situations in which you might feel vulnerable, open, or exposed. The experience of feeling safe enough to share your needs has been distorted, so you don't take relational risks. In some cases, the withdrawal progresses from feelings of loneliness to actually feeling dead or frozen inside. You rarely experience need or dependency. You feel nothing, or you have the sense that something is broken inside.

Movement to task. If trust is damaged, you may also over-invest in tasks related to work, career, school, activities, hobbies, and service. That is, you stay active in the world, but you find it much safer to "do" than to "connect." You may remain energetic, busy, and active in pursuit of good goals, but you stay away from the personal end of life.

Unbalanced "giver" relationships. It is common for a person to be the "giver" in all relationships and to avoid the "receiving." That is, he or she will listen, help, and guide others but keep away from bringing his or her own needs to the table. This often includes codependent relationships as well, in which you rescue and enable others instead of letting them take responsibility for their lives and choices. One of the questions I ask when I am evaluating someone is, "What is the ratio of give and take in your normal lunch conversations? 50–50? 90–10? 10–90?" Usually, when trust has been damaged, it swings toward the 10–90 ratio, as a way for the person to stay safe from being vulnerable.

Bad habits. Trust issues can often lead into troublesome behavior patterns. These can include eating and sleep problems, obsessive behaviors, or addictions.

How do all of these things relate to trust? If you struggle with any of these, it may be that a signal that something needs to be addressed and handled. For example, you probably know people who gain weight while going through a relational crisis. Food is a symptom of the deeper problem.

Fortunately, there are situations in relationships in which trust can be reestablished relatively quickly. For example, if the offending person does something hurtful, but it is not too serious and is a rare or one-time event, all it takes is for the person who experienced the offense to call attention to it: "It made me angry when you dismissed my point of view at the meeting," or "My feelings were hurt when you wouldn't listen to what I was going through with the kids." Those sorts of statements, plus patience and concern, will prompt the other person to see what they have done, mend their ways, reconnect, and move on. These situations are usually glitches, events that aren't a character pattern. They aren't usually something to be concerned about. Sometimes you can even overlook them, as it is to your glory "to overlook an offense" (Proverbs 19:11).

Unfortunately, there are also times when the person's inner character is not what it should be, when the patterns are deeper, and when the trust damage is more serious. These are situations in which appeals for the restoration of the relationship may go ignored, and conversations don't work. That is when you must draw boundaries—for your interests, for the sake of the relationship, and for helping the other person as well. The place and purpose of boundaries is the topic we turn to next.

3

Boundaries and What They Accomplish

When words don't work, boundaries must come next. That is, when an individual doesn't acknowledge the effect of his or her actions on you, you will need to set a limit. The limit protects you from further difficulty, but it also provides an experience for the other person that can be more powerful and have more impact than your words.

A boundary is simply a property line. It clarifies where you end and the other person begins. You form boundaries with your words, with your actions, and sometimes with the help of other people. Boundaries help you to be clear about what you are for and against and what you will and won't tolerate in your relationships.

Two Kinds of Boundaries

To see how setting limits plays out in relationships, it's important to understand that there are two types of boundaries — defining boundaries and protective boundaries. Each kind of boundary has a distinct purpose. It's important that you learn the difference, because defining boundaries should become permanent in your life, while protective boundaries are the ones you can move "beyond."

Defining boundaries are values that establish who you are and who you are not. They are at the core of your identity and reflect what you believe is important and valuable in life. Here are a few examples:

- I follow God and his ways and will always live my life in him.

- I love my family and friends, and I will treat them with grace and truth.

- I will always be growing and will not get off the path.

- I know my mission and purpose in life, and I will not divert from it.

- I say and receive the truth; I'm neither silent in saying it nor defensive in receiving it.

These defining boundaries help you and others know the real you, the person who has substance and stands for things that matter. They help guide your decisions and directions in life.

Here are some examples of how defining boundaries might be used in your relationships:

- "I'm looking for a position that fits my strategic abilities rather than one that is in operations."

- "We have a rule that all who live in this house go to church."

- "I want to hear the truth from you about how you think we are doing in our relationship."

- "I'm a night owl, so let's not plan something that requires that we get up at, oh, dark thirty."

This is simply how you tell people who you are and how they tell you who they are. You clarify and define yourselves with these sorts of boundaries.

Protective boundaries are different. They are designed to "guard your heart" (Proverbs 4:23), and your life, from danger or trouble. There are times when you must protect your values, emotions, gifts, time, and energy from people and situations that may waste or injure them. Protective boundaries have several elements to them. You have to face the reality that talking hasn't fixed a situation, and you have to set a limit.

A protective boundary might begin with a statement like this: "I want us to work this out, but nothing I've said has made any difference, so I'm taking a different route." This affirms that you value the relationship and that you want the other person to understand that your actions are not punitive but, ultimately, redemptive. You are simply trying to solve a difficulty in the relationship with your protective boundaries. The consequences portion of the boundary then needs to be stated in an "If … then …" form to make sure the other person understands you mean business. For example, consider the following statements:

- "If you continue being thirty minutes late to events, I will take a separate car."
- "I need a better work ethic from you in the office, or we'll have to make some changes."
- "If you keep spending over our budget, I will cut up the credit cards."

- "I can't lend you any more money until I see you making serious efforts to find a job."

- "I want to bring your grandkids to see you, but if you just surf the Web while we're there, it's not worth it to come."

- "I want to see my grandkids at times when you don't need a babysitter; otherwise I feel taken advantage of."

- "If you won't stop drinking too much or using drugs, I will take the kids and move out."

Here's the important distinction between a defining boundary and a protective boundary. A defining boundary is forever and unchangeable, part of what makes you "you"; a protective boundary can change if the other person responds to it in a healthy way. Your defining boundaries mean that, for example, you will always follow God, love people, be committed to personal and spiritual growth, and so forth. These are the core parts of you, and you don't change them. But you might change a protective boundary if the other person understands what they are doing to you and makes a significant change. Then you might lessen or end the consequence: no separate cars, no making changes, reissue the credit cards, and so forth. When the change happens, you no longer need the protection.

Here's another way to think about the distinction between defining and protective boundaries. Your skin is like a defining boundary — it's virtually unchanging, except for how you age. It comprises the human cells that, when taken together as a whole, form what most people identify as you. When people see you and say, "There is Jodi," they are observing your skin. In other words, skin is a defining boundary. You don't change your skin. You identify yourself by it.

Now think about the clothes you wear. They protect you

from the elements. In good weather, you wear lighter and fewer clothes. In bad weather, you bundle up. Your clothes change as your need for protection changes. Protective boundaries are like the clothes you need. You adjust them based on how safe you are. In some relationships, you may only need the emotional equivalent of shorts and a T-shirt. And in others, you may need bomb squad gear. Set and keep your defining boundaries—your skin—as a permanent part of who you are. But allow some wiggle room in your protective boundaries.

A couple I worked with had a money problem. The wife was a spendthrift and would not deny herself whatever she could put on her credit cards: clothes, dinners, and online purchases. The habit was not only alienating them but also threatening to ruin their relationship. The husband was constantly afraid that no matter how much he earned and how frugal he was, all their money was going down a hole. After we met, I realized that she did not see how severe the problem was. She said, "He is too worried about tomorrow, and he becomes controlling, and we don't live for today. He doesn't realize that it could all go away tomorrow, and we would not have had a real life. I wish he would understand that." Though the husband was somewhat overly obsessive about money—a marriage misdemeanor—her over-budget spending of thousands per year was a marriage felony.

After I understood the dynamics, I recommended that they separate their finances for a time. He would be in control of his and she of hers. It was a little complicated, but she had a job and an income of her own, and they agreed to the terms. Over time, she experienced the reality of what it was like to live on her own finite income and began to live under budget. At some point, we agreed that they were enough on the same page to do away with the *protective boundary* of the separate finances and to join their financial lives together again. However—and this is the important point—they have agreed that they will always have the *defining boundary* of both submitting to a realistic budget and keeping their mutual spending in line. That will never change.

You Have a Choice, and so Does the Other Person

Anyone, at any time, can reject your boundaries. That is the tough reality. The other person always has a choice. No matter what you say or do, if the other person thinks you're being unfair, unreasonable, unloving, or punitive, and won't change his or her mind about it, you have to accept it. Your choice to have a boundary must be protected, and his or her choice to not agree with yours must also be protected.

For example, I counseled a couple in which the husband, Carl, was verbally harsh and mean to his wife, Jackie. I worked long and hard with him to face his issues, to understand how destructive his actions were to her, and to help him change. But Carl continually minimized his effect on Jackie and blamed her for provoking his anger. Finally, I told them that until Carl "got it," I was concerned about her emotional health. I recommended that whenever he began yelling at her for being ten minutes late for dinner, Jackie should leave the room and, if she had to, the house, until he experienced how deeply he was hurting her. Carl did not agree with my recommended boundary. When Jackie began to act on my recommendation, he got angrier and meaner. And finally, over a long and painful series of events, he found someone else and divorced Jackie.

You may ask if it was worth it for Jackie to set those boundaries and perhaps also wonder if the boundaries themselves caused the breakup. In reality, the problem was not the boundaries. Jackie didn't leave Carl or her commitment to him. She was committed to the relationship and was only protecting herself. Carl was the one who made the choice to leave; she did not force him out. And Jackie's opinion is that, while she was very sad about the loss of the marriage, if she had it all to do over again, she would have still set the boundaries for herself. You don't let another person's relational terrorism threats prohibit you from doing the right thing.

The point is this: your boundaries will create a space, a separation, between you and someone in your life. That person will have a choice to either bridge the separation by making changes and becoming more loving or to increase the distance by moving further away or even leaving the relationship. You can do everything you can to glue things together, but you can never, in your own power, make a person stay with you. Staying or going is always a choice, one that God has given to every person in every area of life: "But if serving the LORD seems undesirable to you, then choose for yourselves this day whom you will serve" (Joshua 24:15). When we love people, we are *for* them, but we set our boundaries against hurtful or dangerous behavior and let them determine their direction — toward us or away from us.

Sometimes people tell me, "Boundaries didn't work for me." They usually mean that when they set a protective limit, the other person blew up or left. But boundaries aren't guaranteed to instill ownership, responsibility, or concern in someone. They can bring reality and clarity. They can protect you. They can show someone the path to change. But boundaries can't remove the other person's choice. So if you look at the real purpose of boundaries from this perspective, they do work. And if you set a boundary and it doesn't have the impact you hoped, I want you to understand that this is still good news. It is diagnostic. It gives you information you need about the character of the other person and the problem you are experiencing. Better to have a doctor's diagnosis for a problem than to avoid making the appointment and allow the problem to do more damage.

When you set and keep good boundaries, you create space and separateness in the relationship that has consequences for the other person; but it's also important to understand that these same boundaries have emotional consequences for you. Sometimes people don't expect the feelings that emerge when they set a limit, and they don't know what to do about that. The next chapter will explain that.

4

The Return of Desire

When our sons were small, they often argued and fought. Their disagreements erupted for any number of reasons: they both wanted the same toy, one wanted to set the rules of a game, or the other teased his brother to the point of insanity. The fights sometimes became physical, but I noticed and intervened when they escalated to the point of "going too far."

Sometimes I simply talked to them, and that was enough to calm matters down. If there was a clearly offending brother, I gave him a consequence: a timeout, the loss of a toy, having to serve his brother. At other times, the best strategy seemed to be to separate them and prohibit contact for a period of time. When it appeared that they had learned a lesson and could once again play well, I let them get together again.

For the situations in which there was a bad guy and I separated them, it would seem to make sense that the hurt brother would have had enough of his offending brother. You would expect that the mean one would want to reconnect and reconcile sooner than the hurt one. But that was not the pattern; there was no pattern. Both boys always wanted to get back together and play after approximately the same amount of time had passed. No matter who was the perpetrator and who the victim, the cooling-off period for each was similar. My best understanding of this is simply that their attachment to each other trumped their desire to be away from each other. After a timeout, their desire to be together was stronger than their anger and fear.

This dynamic doesn't apply just to my sons or even just to kids. It applies to all of us. Understanding the return of desire —the drive to reconnect—is key to learning what happens when you set boundaries.

When There Is Space, There Is Room for Desire

When you set a boundary in a relationship, you create space, room, between you and another person. In healthy connections, the space simply defines you and the other person as two distinct individuals with different minds and opinions, but who still benefit from being connected to each other. You are close, but if one of you is an extrovert and the other is an introvert, for example, the differences don't strain or alienate the relationship. In fact, in healthy relationships, people appreciate the differences: the introvert admires the extrovert's people energy, and the extrovert likes to hear about the interior world of the introvert.

However, when you have to set protective boundaries with someone, the space you create between you is not a celebration of differences. It is about guarding yourself from something not good for you: control or manipulation, for example. And the nature of the space can range from something minor, such as choosing to not talk about certain topics, to something major, such as moving out of your home or even permanently leaving the relationship.

Creating space has an obvious consequence for the other person, but it also has an impact on you. *It can actually increase your desire and interest in a relationship, either the one you are working on, or a new one altogether.* This is ironic, because when you have had a rough go of it with someone, you might think that the last thing you need is any kind of desire for another relationship: *Give me space!* And, while that is a common feeling at the beginning of the boundary period, it does not last forever. The space is a vacuum, and the vacuum puts you in touch with your God-given desire to connect. Especially when there have been trust problems, you look for someone who has your back, who supports your having choices and freedom for your life. By the way, I use the word *desire* in a broader sense than the romantic. The word simply means that you want something: you desire a new car, or tickets to a game, or a promotion, or a good person.

Recognizing the Difference between a Problem and a Solution

The desire to reconnect with your existing relationship or to make a new connection with someone else isn't bad or good in and of itself. The desire can result in a problem or a solution depending on how we respond to it. For example, a woman in my leadership coaching program had a drug addict husband, and she finally put a stop to the behaviors she engaged in that enabled his addiction. She insisted he move out until he got help. That was a good move on her part. Unfortunately, she was vulnerable to his manipulations, and she missed him terribly. Taking advantage of her weakness, he convinced her that he didn't need rehab and that by virtue of his determination and love for her, he was as good as new. She let him move back in, even when those of us in her group begged her not to do it. Things went well, in a honeymoon way, for a few months. Then, when they had an argument over money, he began using again. It took her a great deal more effort, time, and energy this time to establish and maintain a strong boundary with him.

In this woman's case, the desire for reconnection resulted in a problem, but desire itself wasn't the problem. The problem was that she gave in to the desire too quickly, not realizing he wasn't ready yet.

But there are other occasions when responding to desire leads to a good result. I know, for example, a husband whose wife cheated on him and almost ended the marriage. He was devastated for a long time. Though he could have divorced her and no one would have blamed him, he still loved her and wanted to heal the relationship. She agreed to leave the other man, and she and her husband went through an extensive process of personal growth, both individually and in their relationship.

At the beginning of their recommitment to repairing the connection, he felt no love for her, no positive feelings. The only emotions he could experience were hurt and anger. He felt detached and guarded, unable to trust her. He wasn't trying to punish his wife by avoiding her; he truly cared about her, at least objectively, as a person and wanted the best for her. From a values standpoint, he loved her. But the emotions of wanting, longing, and missing, much less being "in love," were simply nonexistent.

Fortunately, she responded to this by understanding and owning the depth of the wound she had created in him. She was not only remorseful but also patient. She told him, "I'll do whatever it takes for as long as it takes for us to reconnect," and she did. In time and with the work they did, he began to open up inside. He grew, he learned, and he healed. And gradually, he began to miss the connection they had. The space between them became an unpleasant emptiness for him, and he was able to take the relational risks that enabled them to begin drawing closer to each other as a couple.

Here is the point: wanting someone doesn't mean you are crazy for having the desire, nor that the time is necessarily right to reconnect with the person. It is simply a sign that you are alive inside and that the boundary has given you breathing room to feel your human need for connection. Pay attention to it, be glad you are alive, and use good judgment and good people to help you decide what to do with it.

Healthy Responses to the New Desire

When you want to reconnect, it can mean good things are happening inside you. Here are some examples.

A new romantic relationship. After a divorce or a season of withdrawing from dating, you may find yourself waking up inside again. You might imagine what it would be like to get to know someone who is interesting to you or interested in you. You may feel a sense of cautious optimism that a new person could be a fresh start and that things can be better for you.

The same romantic relationship. You may be more open

to starting over with your current connection. Like my sons, your need for the attachment has kicked back in; you miss the good parts of the relationship and feel more hopeful that perhaps things can change. You want to put effort and life back into it, making it what you hoped it could have been originally.

The same friend or family member. In the nonromantic area of life, it could be that your history and involvement with this person gives you a renewed sense that you'd like to try to make it work. For example, an adult child will sometimes distance herself from an unhealthy parent for a period of time and then begin thinking about trying things again. Or estranged friends will call each other to work things out, realizing the connection is larger than the problem they had.

It can take a short time or a long time for the desire to emerge. After a minor disconnect, you may miss the other person in a few hours or days and call to work things out. If the situation is serious and damaging, it can take much longer. For example, some people swear off dating for a long time when their trust and desire have been buried under years of fear or painful memories. I counseled a man who, after a painful divorce, threw himself into his work and his friendships for several years. He did not miss dating at all. Whenever he considered it, his first thought was, "It's not worth it." For most of us, however, in time and with the right amount of safety, normality, and healthy friendships and activities, the longing for relationship does reoccur.

All of these are examples of a healthy response to the reemergence of desire. After a relational disappointment, it is natural and good to fill up your life with people who can be there with and for you. In fact, if you try setting boundaries in a vacuum—without relational support from others—it usually results in a disaster.

Unhealthy Responses to the New Desire

Distancing yourself from someone without having anywhere else to go relationally makes it more likely that you will compromise your boundaries by returning to or giving greater power to your difficult person. Jesus' parable of spirits and an empty house echoes this truth:

> When an impure spirit comes out of a person, it goes through arid places seeking rest and does not find it. Then it says, "I will return to the house I left." When it arrives, it finds the house unoccupied, swept clean and put in order. Then it goes and takes with it seven other spirits more wicked than itself, and they go in and live there. (Matthew 12:43–45)

Though Jesus' story is about the need for spiritual rejuvenation, the principle is the same: after a relational difficulty, if you set limits but are empty inside, you are even more vulnerable to allowing a toxic or untimely relationship into your life. For example, my friends Ken and Laura had major struggles with Leslie, their teenage daughter. Leslie snuck out at all hours of the night to go to parties where alcohol and drugs were available. They tried counseling, but Leslie's condition was too serious. Finally, Ken and Laura put her in a therapeutic boarding school that had specialized help for her. The couple was relieved. Leslie's behavior had made them miserable during the past two years.

However, as soon as Leslie arrived at the school, she called and emailed her parents over and over again, begging them to let her come home, saying she was lonely and missed them. These messages penetrated to the space inside Ken and Laura, where they were beginning to miss her presence, and they finally let her come home after six weeks, which was a few months early. The results were disastrous. Within a month, Leslie was acting out again. Finally, the couple had to send her away again, and this time they required that she stay for the entire period.

Did Leslie miss her parents? Certainly. I think she really loved and was attached to them. She was not faking the relationship. But she was not ready or healthy enough yet. It was Ken and Laura's empty space inside, mixed with some parental guilt, that drove them to the unhealthy choice.

Approach-avoidance. As with the husband who struggled to rekindle a desire to reconnect with his wife after she had an affair, many people have a very difficult time when desire reemerges. They feel the need for connection, but they can't respond to it. The engine is running, but the car stays in neutral. Psychologists call this the "approach-avoidance conflict." problem. Two separate drives are at war within your skin. One says, "I want to get closer," and the other says, "Warning, danger!" And you feel pulled back and forth between the two.

In fact, you may even wish the desire would go away, because it is less disruptive and painful. But once desire has returned after you have protected yourself with boundaries, it is hard to put the genie back into the bottle. It is actually a sign of health and an indication that you are coming back to life emotionally.

Most of us have made a few mistakes along the way when the desire comes back. It's not the end of the world, but it can slow down your move beyond boundaries. My best recommendation is to stay in contact and be real with a few mature people who care for you and will tell you the truth. This can help you refrain from making serious errors and commitments before you are ready.

Banish Victimhood

When you begin to move beyond self-protection and reenter the world of trusting again, be aware of a tendency to see yourself as a victim. It is a common response to a bad relationship, but it won't get you into the healthier connections you are looking for. Victimhood is characterized by three tendencies: *a sense of globalized helplessness to act and make things better, a focus on the "bad other,"* and *the perception of moral superiority.* Let's unpack these.

Global helplessness. You feel you have no choices, that others "make" you do things you don't want to do. Global helplessness can result from negative experiences beyond your control. When you are emotionally invested in someone, whether it be in business, romance, or friendship, you often allow the other person a disproportionate influence on your thoughts, feelings, and choices. Sometimes the line between trust and control is blurred, and you allow their perceptions to determine your choices more than you should.

This dynamic creates a sense of helplessness, a feeling that you cannot choose to protect yourself when you are around someone you care about. The codependent wife of an alcoholic is a good example. When he is sober, he apologizes tearfully and promises it will never happen again. And against her better judgment and values, the wife gives in to his manipulation, only to later regret it. This reinforces her sense of, "I have no choices and no power." I see this happen in the workforce as well, especially when someone reports to a controlling boss. The person feels hemmed in by the micro-managing and, in reality, has limited choices in the first place, because he is dealing with a boss. The result is a sense of futility, as in "Why try?"

Do not give in to the helpless position. You don't have infinite choices, as none of us is God. But unless someone has a gun to your head, you have some choices. For example, in the case of the controlling boss, I have worked with professionals who first had to learn to have the tough conversations with their superior. Then they had to have another meeting with the boss and the boss's boss followed by a meeting with the HR department. It is time-consuming, but the process is designed to work. Maximize your choices, do it the hard way, and don't give in to global helplessness.

Focus on the "bad other." This is a tendency to see one's problems, difficulties, and sometimes one's entire life through the lens of how hurtful the other person was. When you go through a set of bad experiences with someone, it leaves unpleasant memories. To deal with this and resolve it, we all need a season of protest in which we allow ourselves to hate what happened to us and renounce it. Basically, you need to say, "Ouch, I don't like this; why did this happen to me?" It is a form of confession or agreeing with the truth of an experience. Protest gets the matter out in front of you and into relationship with those who can understand and support you.

This is how we all begin to connect, recover, and grow from our experiences; we cannot heal from what we do not confess and protest. David protested vigorously when he encountered his own difficult times: "Why, LORD, do you stand far off? Why do you hide yourself in times of trouble?" (Psalm 10:1). He gave voice to his negative feelings and pain.

However, the protest is limited to a season. It has a beginning and an end. Once protest has served its purpose, it then moves into acceptance of reality and integration of that reality into life. We recover, learn, and move on. Sometimes, however, people refuse to terminate this phase and find that it is not a season, but a permanent condition. That is, they get stuck putting time, energy, and focus into how bad the other person was. Their thoughts, memories, and conversations are loaded with references to this individual and his or her destructiveness.

I was once at a party and met a couple who had been married for a year. The husband had previously been through a painful divorce. Within the first ten minutes of our conversation, he mentioned three times what a nightmare his ex had been. He always phrased things in ways that were intended to appear as compliments about his new wife, but that's not how it came out. For example, "It's been so much better with Stacy than it ever was with Beth," or "After what I've been through, I really appreciate Stacy." But it was actually embarrassing, and I felt sorry for his new wife. I could imagine that she would have preferred to have been affirmed for herself and not in contrast to someone else. But clearly this man had not finished his protest of the bad other. It was not just a season for him; he was in danger of victimhood becoming his identity—a condition that could and likely would undermine his new marriage as well.

Your closest friends will listen, support, and encourage you when you are getting the protest out of your system. But they will not be patient forever. An endless season of venting isn't good for you either. Focusing on the bad other takes up entirely too much space in your life and mind and inhibits your ability to find new people and opportunities.

The perception of moral superiority. You know you've entered the world of victimhood when you focus on your moral superiority to the other person. You see her as a bad person, or at least not as good as yourself. You may concentrate on the thought that he was 90 percent or even 100 percent of the problem. For example, a betrayed wife may think, *I would never do to him what he did to me.* Thoughts like these, though they may be true, can cause you problems.

The reason the perception of moral superiority doesn't help you is that it prevents growth and great relationships. It inhibits personal growth because growth requires humility. A focus on being the good guy doesn't provide a great deal of incentive to look at your issues and change. And healthy people tend to avoid those who are stuck in the morally superior position. Nobody wants to walk through life with someone who is invested in being the good guy; it's hard to be open and real with that kind of person.

I once worked with a couple, for example, where the wife was more concerned about being right than she was in being connected to her husband. When they disagreed, he was willing to look at his side and own where he might be off base. She, however, argued to death even the smallest matters, such as why they were late to a session, to avoid being wrong. She persisted even when she knew doing so alienated her husband.

So if you are, in reality, the good guy or even the innocent party in the relational conflict, let that be something you are aware of. Be happy you didn't partake deeply of the dysfunction. That is a good thing and speaks well for you. At the same time, be willing to take on a humble attitude of being a learner and a grower. Don't put your energies into your moral superiority. It will not benefit you in any way. And on a deeper level, it helps to remember that, though you may have been mistreated by another, there is no place for moral superiority for any of us. Ultimately, a high price has already been paid for the moral debt all of us owe: "For Christ also suffered once for sins, the righteous for the unrighteous" (1 Peter 3:18).

The Antidotes to Victimhood

I have seen the three just-mentioned characteristics of victimhood keep people miserable and make those around them miserable as well. Stay away from the victim stance. Instead, be a person who owns your choices, pays attention to your life, and chooses to remain in the humble position. Here are some suggestions to help.

Forgive and be forgiven. If you've been wronged by a business relationship or a family member has let you down, cancel the debt and let it go. Forgiveness for the Christian is the norm: "Be kind and compassionate to one another, forgiving each other, just as in Christ God forgave you" (Ephesians 4:32). But just as importantly, search out anything you might need to be forgiven of as well. There may be nothing at all you did wrong, but it's worth looking into.

Perhaps you looked the other way when a problem happened, and you didn't confront it. Or maybe you didn't go after advice from people who would have told you to avoid the relationship. But on a larger scale, simply be a confessional, repentant person in general. That is, be open to God telling you that you make mistakes on a daily basis, irrespective of the difficult relationship. It's good for your soul. My experience with the victim role is that the less a person sees they need to receive forgiveness, the stronger the victimhood. But when they begin to see the contributions they made to their own misery and ask forgiveness, the stronghold begins to loosen.

Be proactive. Take initiative, take the first step, in all areas of life: financial, relational, career, family, personal, and spiritual. Figure out what you want, set goals, and make plans. This is a proactive life, and it will go a long way to resolving victimhood for you. Once you experience the adrenalin rush of taking positive initiative and the sense of power and freedom it creates, global helplessness begins to dissipate.

Move from "should have" to what's real. Focusing on what should have happened keeps victims stuck: *I should have gotten the promotion. My dad should have affirmed me. My kids should have appreciated me.* This gets you nowhere, because the "should have" is an ideal that didn't happen. Focusing on the real and actual will help.

Look at it as learning to solve problems: *I will figure out why I didn't get the promotion and get it next time. I will gain the affirmation of a mature man and use that to finish what my dad didn't do. I will be happy with the fact that my kids are doing OK in life, even if they don't give me any credit.* These steps will give you a fresh sense of life that will help you leave victimhood behind.

PART 2

KNOWING WHEN YOU'RE READY

During one of my routine workouts at the gym, I lifted an upper-body weight at an awkward angle and felt a sharp shoulder pain. I didn't think a lot about it, but in the next few days, it didn't go away. I checked in with a physical therapist, who told me I had pulled a muscle. He prescribed stretches and a few weeks of laying off the upper-body work. I didn't mind the stretches, but as the days away from weight training wore on, I became impatient. I didn't like feeling as if I was losing ground, so I rushed the calendar and did an upper-body workout again. This time the pain was even sharper.

It's no surprise that I ended up back in the office of my physical therapist. After a lecture, he told me, "You're headed for surgery if you don't get serious about this." Then he doubled the amount of time off from the weights. This time, I paid attention and stayed away from exerting those muscles.

In a similar way, you may have a tendency to jump the gun in your relational life. Sometimes people rebound and jump into the wrong new relationship; other times they become involved too soon; at still other times they trust someone before it is time to trust. When a relationship seems to have potential, the connection is going well, and the desires are strong, you don't move in a "ready-aim-fire" sequence. It is more like "fire-fire-fire." And then the second recovery time is much longer, as was the case with my shoulder.

Or perhaps you're in the opposite camp. You may be so mistrustful that, even though you experience the desire for connection, you talk yourself out of it, stay busy and uninvolved, and basically ward off taking any moves toward a deeper connection. In this case, instead of the ready-aim-fire sequence, you might be prone to "ready-ready-ready," or maybe even "never ready."

Or maybe you have both tendencies, swinging from high caution to throwing caution to the wind and then swinging back again to caution. We all have some of these tendencies. But what helps is having a way to know when, inside yourself, you are ready to begin opening up again on a more vulnerable level to another person. The chapters in part 2 provide guidelines to help you determine that. Each chapter describes a marker of growth, one that indicates whether you have a green light to move ahead or a warning flag indicating you need to move cautiously or stop completely. Here is the benefit: *you want to be as ready as possible to find and conduct the best relationships possible.* It is worth learning how to do these steps.

5

You Admit the Hurt
and Receive Support

Nobody wants to be a wimp or a whiner. The idea of being a high-maintenance complainer, running to friends with the gory details of every relational problem, would drive most of us to consider taking a vow of silence. Take it from Don Draper, the secretive lead character in the TV show *Mad Men,* who said to a psychologist doing research for his company, "Why does everybody need to talk about everything?" We are averse to airing our personal laundry in public.

You may feel like many people who, after a hard relationship, simply want to get it behind them and move on without a lot of discussion. In fact, some people are averse to talking about their painful relationship because they feel it gives the difficult person even more power and control over their lives; they don't want to waste any more of themselves on the person than they have to. Having said that, however, *if you fail to admit the hurt you've experienced and receive support, you will remain unable to fully reconnect with anyone else.* It's just that simple.

To have a hope of an intimate, healthy relationship in the future, you have to clean up the emotional wounds from the difficult relationship in your past. You don't need to talk about every detail of what happened, but if the relationship was important to you, you simply must talk about it with a few safe people for some period of time.

When a relationship goes the wrong way, you experience some sort of wounding inside. It may be mild, moderate, or severe, but there is hurt. You may feel used, let down, controlled, or put down, depending on what has happened. But it is a thoroughly negative experience. In and of itself, the existence of the wound is not a bad thing. In fact, it is a sign that you are alive and that the person meant something to you. If the person you love most looked at you and said, "I don't want you anymore," and you thought, *Oh well, that's a choice you have a right to make,* with no emotional response, that is a problem. Either you never really connected with that person in the first place or something is broken inside you. Problems with love and relationships should feel bad—and that is good.

But wounds should not stay wounds. They need to heal. A relational wound needs to be resolved so that you get back to normal life—that is, being in healthy connections, being freed from the past, and exercising your gifts and passions. And don't depend on the old proverb that says, "Time heals all wounds," because it's not true. Time, by itself, heals very little. Broken bones need more than time, as do homes in disrepair and lives that have had a troubled relationship. What you really need in order to heal is support. If it is relationship that wounded you, it is relationship that is required to heal you.

When you let someone know the nature of your hurt, you

allow yourself to open up and be vulnerable. By telling another human being the facts and feelings about what you experienced, you give up the perception of being self-sufficient and emotionally impenetrable. In the presence of another, you acknowledge the reality that you suffered and receive support.

Expressing weakness isn't just an emotional download; it has a twofold purpose. First, it brings your hurts out of isolation, where they would otherwise fester and make things worse. Second, it draws those hurts into a relational sphere, where care and support can repair the damage.

This may mean that you may have to revisit the most painful parts of the relationship and not move on too quickly. If you are an action-oriented person, this may seem like a backward step. But in reality, it is a forward step. The process of revisiting the past enables you to clear the decks of the previous relationship so you don't carry old emotional junk into a new relationship.

My friend Jennifer is the kind of person who is all about forward motion. A small-business owner who hits life hard and gets things done, her positive, high-energy approach motivates her employees and is key to her success. When her husband, Scott, out of the blue told her he had found someone else and was ending the marriage, Jennifer didn't have the skills she needed to handle such a profound betrayal. So she tried to deal with the crisis in the same way she approached her work. She sat down and had extensive conversations with Scott, trying to dissuade him from the other woman. She even tried to negotiate and came up with a written plan for fixing the marriage.

However, it takes two people to reconcile. Scott was on his way out and was not open to Jennifer's thoughts. After he left, she tried to stay positive and busy and threw herself into her work more than usual. However, she soon found herself unable to run the business at the same high-energy levels she had before. She began losing interest in her work, her concentration wavered, and she even made some strategic financial blunders.

As her friend, I finally said, "You can't be the strong one here. You are simply going to have to unpack the feelings with someone." Jennifer resisted this for a number of reasons. She didn't want to bother others. She was concerned that she would get depressed and lose her positive outlook. She didn't want to be seen as weak. But finally, after all her attempts to get back on track via willpower and trying harder failed, she agreed.

With a few safe friends, Jennifer opened up and shared how shattered she actually was by Scott's leaving. It was no surprise to them. They had asked her how she was doing when the crisis began, and she had quickly minimized the pain. But not this time. And though it was painful to bring the wounds into her relationships with others, Jennifer experienced a great sense of relief, comfort, and companionship when she did so.

That was the beginning of Jennifer's journey out of her failed marriage. Had she not allowed others in, she would likely now be a depressed, lonely workaholic instead of the vibrant person she is today.

If you're like Jennifer, you need to get beyond the tendency to minimize, be the strong one, and go it alone. You are far better off when you allow the antibiotics of supportive relationships to salve those internal wounds where the infection resides. But I know it isn't easy.

I once coached Allan, a businessman who had a broken relationship with his father. It was significant for his emotional life, and for his professional life as well. While Allan's dad had been a hardworking man, he was also critical of his son's success and even threatened by it. He did not want his son to excel beyond his own level of career success and was threatened by the accomplishments and potential of a bright and gifted boy. When the boy became an adult, any time he had a small failure in his business, he experienced intense shame and humiliation, a deep attack on himself. These experiences were so painful that Allan hid his failures from others and even from himself. Of course, this also kept him from learning from failure, dealing opening with it, and moving on successfully in his field. He was not reaching anywhere near his potential as a businessman.

At the same time, Allan remained loyal to his dad and all the training his father had given him. So it was difficult for him to admit negative feelings of hurt and anger about his dad. He didn't want to dishonor his father. And when he occasionally did share something with others about the difficulties of his relationship with his dad, he inevitably cut them off if they expressed any empathy, saying, "It's okay; things are fine now." People were confused by this; they were drawn into his story but then felt rebuffed by his dismissals.

This teeter-tottering between acknowledging his pain and then minimizing it reflected the battle he experienced within. As much as Allan wanted to tell the truth about his relational hurt with his dad, he didn't want his dad to be the bad guy. I brought this pattern to his attention and said, "You already do honor your dad. But when you avoid telling the whole truth, you dishonor him by creating a person that did not exist." He got that and was then able to allow the whole story to come out. When he was finally able to share his experiences, the people in his life who cared about him were able to support and empathize with him. And in the course of time, Allan's professional performance reached levels much closer to his actual abilities.

This is a hard step to take, but once you begin the process of opening up, you may find that it's not as hard as it once seemed. You are designed to connect. It actually feels good to allow others access to the painful places within you. Admit the hurt and receive the support, and you are on the way.

6

You Understand
Your Own Past Choices

Difficult relationships tend to provide us with more teaching moments than do routine relationships. The trouble difficult relationships cause in our lives creates a sharp focus on the connection and what went wrong. This is a good thing, actually. If you spend time and energy figuring out what went wrong, you are less likely to make the same mistake again. On a deeper level, you will know yourself and others in a clear and helpful way.

Whenever I talk with people about their relationships, one of the first subjects I ask them to talk about is a painful relationship from the past. They are often hesitant to do this, either because they don't understand the purpose it serves (*Why should I think about this? It's in the past. I need to move on*), or because they fear the pain it might bring up (*Don't make me go back there; there are dark memories I don't want to revisit*). However, the people I coach need to learn from their past relational choices—and so do you. In fact, you ignore them at your peril. If you fail to do the work described in this chapter, I can virtually guarantee that you will repeat your past mistakes in a future relationship.

In guiding people through a process of examining a previous difficult relationship, the one question I have found most helpful is this: *What was the payoff in your choice?* In other words, what did you think you were getting when you began a relationship with this person?

You picked your difficult person for a reason — there was something you valued and wanted and hoped for. And because the need was strong, you *may not have paid attention to something else in that person's character.* You either minimized or denied some sign, some reality, some warning light that all was not well. And the character issue ended up being a bigger deal than you thought.

Of course, there are relationships in which little or no choice is involved: a parent, a sibling, or a coworker. In these situations, you didn't do the selecting; it was done for you. However, it is still helpful to think about how you may have allowed, ignored, or been in denial about the person's negative traits *within the context of the relationship.* For example, suppose you work with someone who is always asking you to bail him out when he doesn't get reports in on time. Think about the times you may have rescued him from his own irresponsibility and why you did that. Did you want to keep the peace? Did you feel sorry for him? Did you think that if you helped him one last time, he would become more responsible?

A helpful approach to understanding your past choices is first to take a look at the character of the person with whom you have had trouble. Character problems drive the attitudes and behaviors that cause trouble in a relationship. After that, look at the payoff. The payoff is *the benefit you hoped to gain by putting up with the person's character.* We simply have a tendency to ignore bad behavior if there is something important we need from the person.

Identify the Character Problems

I mentioned that we tend to miss the character problems in someone we are interested in. By the word "character," I don't mean integrity, morality, or faith in God. That is the usual understanding of the word. I define character as *that set of abilities we need to meet the demands of reality*. Reality demands that we handle many things: relationships, love, conflicts, problems, losses, finances, our mission in life, and self-care, to name a few. It takes abilities and skills to handle what life throws our way. Abilities such as the capacity to connect at deep levels, to be honest, to set healthy boundaries, and to accept and adapt to the losses in our lives are examples.

So when I talk about character problems, I mean the deficits in those abilities, which get in the way of love and intimacy, not to mention growth. Here are a few examples:

- Deception
- Emotional unavailability
- Control
- Manipulation
- Excuses
- Blame
- A victim stance
- Irresponsibility
- Distrust
- Condemnation
- Self-absorption
- Narcissism

Review this list for a moment and think about it. No one in their right mind would sign up to fall in love with or invest in a life with someone who exhibited these traits. These are *bad things.* They hurt, they alienate, and they ruin relationships and people.

Yet we do sign up for them, every day. You can probably think of a few people who have several of these traits, people you have trusted or with whom you have been vulnerable. Why? *Because you were not in your right mind.* Truly. You were disconnected from reality, in a state of temporary insanity. I don't mean you need antipsychotic medication. I mean that you ignored some truth about the person's wiring. And it has to do with the payoff. The payoff you were attracted to blinded you to the truth of what was really going on.

Sometimes people will say things like, "It was out of the blue. He was nice to me, and then he turned on me." In their experience, a switch was pulled and day became night, with no warning. The person feels jolted and worked over and sometimes goes into a state of shock. The reality, however, is that *character issues are never sudden. They take time to develop and are long-standing patterns.* There is no switch. The patterns were there all along, but your desire for the relationship blinded you.

Certainly, if the difficult person is a trauma victim and suffers from post-traumatic stress disorder, that might make sense. Trauma sufferers have flashbacks, sudden mood swings, and emotional instability. If that is the case, you need to have compassion on the person and chalk up the misery to the trauma. But most relational problems are character based, not trauma based. High levels of selfishness, control, or irresponsibility, for example, are not the usual results of trauma. So be sure to distinguish between character and trauma.

Name the Payoff

By payoff, I mean the traits and abilities in others that we think will make life better for us. They are positive aspects of a person's psyche that we are drawn to or feel we need. Our longing for them dulls our awareness of that person's darker side. Here are a few examples. For some period of time in the relationship, the person had the following:

- *Warmth:* she was gentle and nurturing with me
- *Affirmation:* he saw the good in me
- *Safety:* he did not condemn or judge me
- *Structure:* she was organized and got things done
- *Humor:* she helped lighten the burdens and cheered me up
- *A great family:* his relatives were much healthier than mine
- *Drive:* she was focused and knew where she was going
- *Initiative:* she took risks and was brave in making decisions
- *Competency:* he was talented, and I needed his talent in my organization
- *People skills:* he handled people better than I did, so I depended on him
- *Intelligence:* she was smart, and I needed smarts in my department

In the toughest cases, the trait is simply that *he liked me.* That is, sometimes people feel so alone and desperate that they are grateful just for someone to be pursuing them, no matter what that person's character may be.

However this plays out, the payoff is that *the desired good negated the bad*.

People in sales know how to maximize the good and minimize the bad in a product or service. A high-powered car salesman knows how to spin the truth so that a car that has limited horsepower is described as "safe and economical"; an unsafe street machine is "exciting and fun." We have a similar kind of ability to spin the truth when it comes to our relationships. When we want something badly enough, we ignore reality. Love is not blind, but desire can be.

Here are some examples of payoffs:

- You allowed him to control you because you were weak and afraid.

- You ignored detachment and disconnection because she was a nice person.

- You minimized irresponsibility because she had a great personality and charm.

- You let him into your life because you were compliant and guilt-based, and he was free and a rebel.

- You put up with his tendency to divide people on the team because he was a good strategist.

- You didn't pay attention to childishness because she was needy, and you felt protective.

Do you see how the payoff works? It is an insidious process. It tends to occur slowly over time. The good aspects are generally apparent and right out there. The bad ones don't come out until later, when the ether wears off and the honeymoon is over. We are simply not aware of the payoff while we are in the middle of the relationship. Instead, we are focused on solving problems, improving things, questioning our own judgment, and trying to be positive about it all. It's not until later, after we have some distance, that we can gain clarity and perspective on the true dynamics of what went on.

Here are a few guidelines to help you review your relationship and gain some helpful insights about it:

- What drew me to this person?
- What led me to think this person had what I needed?
- When did I first notice a significant problem in the relationship?
- How did I minimize the problem in order to get the good from the person?
- What was the result of minimizing the problem?

The information you gather here will help you avoid these issues in future relationships.

This doesn't mean that the other person has some plan or agenda to hook you in. This occurs sometimes, but certainly not always. Most of the time, difficult people are responding to their own issues but remain unaware of them or the impact they have on others. I say this to prevent you from feeling like you were sucked into a trap. Most of the time, both parties are in a dysfunctional dance, and neither one knows what's going on. The difference now is that you can choose to stop dancing so that your future will be better than your past!

Be a Student of Your Poor Choices

The prospect of studying your poor relational choices or your tendencies to put up with bad behavior longer than you should have is not exciting. It's painful and can even be a bit embarrassing to do the sort of relational autopsy I am recommending.

But it is also exceedingly helpful. When the lights come on and you see your relational patterns, you have greater ability to make improved choices. Not only that, but you are more able to meet your relational needs *while at the same time not sabotaging yourself in a blind pursuit of the payoff.*

That is huge. In other words, you can have it all. You can find interesting, caring, and strong people, and there is no reason in the world that you must at the same time be leveraged into accepting dark character traits. Certainly no one is perfect, and finding a perfect person is not the goal. But perfect is a long way from dark. My goal for you is that you will be enlightened and empowered to choose people who are both good and good for you.

Here is an example of how this whole process works —from identifying character problems to naming the payoff and being a student of one's poor choices. Michelle, a woman I worked with, had a long-standing history of picking men who were nice but needy. They tended to be somewhat passive, yet they were nevertheless good-hearted people. Her most recent dating relationship lasted several years, and she finally became concerned that it wasn't going anywhere. Michelle became close to the man, and then something inside compelled her to pull away. She backed off for a while, only to return again later.

Michelle had great difficulty in resolving her particular relational pattern for two reasons. One was that she was a kind person and had a lot of personal grace and empathy. She gave people the benefit of the doubt. The niceness of the men she chose made her more long-suffering than she should have been. She thought well of them and hoped that they would grow into the person she needed or that she would accept what was there and commit.

The second reason was that her father had been highly critical of her and only drew close when she performed well. When the grades were good and she excelled in athletics and music, Dad was affirming. But he cut off the affection and became cold and picky when Michelle made mistakes or let him see her imperfections. Because of this old pattern, she developed a deep hunger for unconditional acceptance from a man.

The man she was currently dating was very accepting and warm toward her real self, who she really was. He truly loved Michelle when she was needy or imperfect. This was like an oasis in her emotional desert, and so she couldn't walk away. At the same time, however, the healthy part of her wanted a man who wasn't so needy and who was as strong as she was. She continued going back and forth in the relationship, getting close to a commitment and then backing off.

As the pattern became clearer to her, Michelle was able to gradually free herself from the back-and-forth dance. She also developed some male buddies, that is, nondating friendships. Because they were men who were warm and strong, they helped fill the holes left by her own dad. This decreased the draw to find a dad in her romantic life, and she was more able to be objective about what she wanted in a man. Michelle was able to finally say good-bye to her difficult relationship, not because the person she was dating was a bad man, but because the relationship was not right for her.

Here is the point: *the extent to which you see and own the relational pattern you were stuck in is the extent to which you can move beyond boundaries. Be as brutally honest and objective as you can. Get perspective from others. The more you go after reality, the more you will free yourself from the patterns that have kept you stuck.*

7

You Can Connect
the Dots

Relational patterns have a parent, and that parent is the past.
The patterns I wrote about in the last chapter do not emerge
from thin air. They have roots in older, more established, significant relationships, sometimes from childhood and sometimes in adulthood. Over time, the better you can connect
the dots — between past and present — the freer you will be
to move on beyond your protective boundaries into the risks
involved with intimacy.

Think, for example, about who you are as a person now:
your values, interests, and life directions. Your significant
relationships most likely played a major part in who you have
become. If you love to teach, a relative who worked in edu-
cation or one of your teachers may have inspired you. If you
have a drive for running an organization, most likely someone took you under his or her wing and encouraged you to
learn and grow in leadership.

I relied on this connect-the-dots dynamic when I recently
consulted with the board of a large charity organization

that works with children in need. I led a weekend retreat to help the board members establish deeper connections to the organization's mission and values and to help them work better together as a team.

When we met, I talked to them about where passion arises and pointed out that most of the time it comes from relationships. Most people don't donate to a charity, much less commit to board membership, based on a mission statement or a key values document. People are busy and have great demands on their time. Something personal has to resonate in order for an individual to commit time, energy, and money to an organization. Concepts don't drive that kind of commitment; relationship does. We commit to causes and organizations because of how they intersect with our own life experience. On a flipchart, I wrote some examples of how that might have happened for the members of this particular board:

- Your parents were "kid people," and your home was a central space for your friends to hang out.

- You knew kids in your neighborhood or school whose family situations were destructive and painful.

- Your church had a strong outreach to kids in need, and you were exposed to it.

- As an adult, you were involved in helping and coaching kids.

- A friend invited you to a fundraiser for a charity, and you were moved by the stories told at the event.

- You experienced neglect or abuse in your home growing up, and you have always been sensitive to others who experience the same thing.

The retreat agenda was twofold: to connect people to their own stories about kids at risk and to connect the board members to each other so that they would function at a higher level as a team. I gave everyone an exercise. I said, "Look at this list for a moment and see if any of these stories fit you. You may come up with something not on the list. Think about what first got your attention about this charity on a personal level. And then we'll go around the room and tell each other our stories."

One by one, people gave their narratives. One had a story of a friend in trouble. One benefited from families who had reached out. One was touched by an appeal at a dinner party. One had personally suffered mistreatment. But as people shared, you could see them connecting the dots between their past experiences and their present values. They were returning to the roots of why they had made the commitments that they had, and their decisions made more sense to them. At the same time, they looked at each other and recognized commonalities: "I didn't know that about you." "I had a very similar experience to yours." "I've known you for a long time on this board, and I never understood what attracted you to this involvement."

In this chapter, you will learn how to craft your own narrative in a way that helps provide perspective on your difficult relationships. This understanding is a path to freedom in any present and future connections you have.

What's Your Relational Narrative?

Just as members of the board of directors had narratives about their charity commitments, you have a narrative about your relational commitments. Your narrative affects how you relate today, but it did not suddenly begin with your problematic relationship. It sprang from the soil of the early connections that formed and influenced how you act, feel, and think in your relationships. Of course, the earlier the relationships, such as in your family of origin, the more influence this narrative has on who you are and how you relate to others.

In fact, it might even be that your troublesome relationship is with a parent, sibling, or someone from your childhood. And the more severe the problems, the more influence your narrative will have on your present relationships. We learn about love, intimacy, control, and reality from those closest to us. Though we ultimately make our own choices, we are deeply marked, for good or for bad, by those who matter to us.

You may have heard that you become like those you are with and take on their characteristics. The psychological term for this is *fusion*. Fusion happens when an individual takes on the same problems experienced in his or her family. For example, an alcoholic family produces an alcoholic adult child. But there are also exceptions to this. Sometimes we react in *opposition* to the way we were treated in an effort to separate ourselves from the toxicity we experienced or because we are determined not to be like the people who wounded us. We *react against*. That's how the neat freak arises from the cluttered home and the rebel emerges from the overcontrolling environment.

We all have some kind of response to our formative environment. Sometimes we take on the troublesome characteristics we grew up with, and sometimes we react against them. When it comes to relationships, neither approach offers a real solution, though the person who acts in opposition can at least identify that there is a problem to solve. But neither response by itself will fix the root problem. This is because both stances are *fear-based, not growth-based.*

Fusion is about fear. It occurs when a person adopts the family dysfunctions out of fear of going against one's parents and/or disagreeing with them. For example, he doesn't want to alienate himself from the family or become angry himself. Reacting in opposition to family dysfunctions is also fear-based. She is afraid of being swallowed up and engulfed in a sick system, losing herself, so she does a 180-degree turn away from the patterns of her parents.

Here are some examples of family dynamics and how a person might respond with either fusion or opposition. As you review the list, see if you resonate with any of these scenarios. Note that sometimes several patterns can be active simultaneously so it's possible you could relate to more than one.

Dynamic: Your parents were nice people but discouraged honesty, confrontation, and anger.

Fusion: You avoid confrontation and often seem to find yourself with angry or controlling people.

Opposition: You become angry too quickly and are overly confrontational with others.

Dynamic: Your family was somewhat rigid and black-and-white in their values and basic rules of life.

Fusion: You have difficulty with the unknown, with complexity, and with loose ends, such as problems that won't be resolved quickly.

Opposition: You are so driven to explore every option that you have a hard time making commitments to get things done.

Dynamic: You experienced good structure and care in your family, but your family didn't talk about feelings or relational issues.

Fusion: You live in the world of the mind and are uncomfortable with the emotional side of life.

Opposition: You are so emotional that your feelings sometimes get you in trouble.

Dynamic: You had a parent who was loving but irresponsible or unreliable.

Fusion: You have difficulty taking responsibility for your life and give control of it to others.

Opposition: You had to grow up quickly and became overresponsible and guilt-ridden.

Dynamic: You had chaos in your home.

Fusion: You find yourself unable to meet goals, finish projects, and have structure in your life.

Opposition: You have become rigid and let your schedule get in the way of relationships.

Dynamic: You had an immature parent.

Fusion: You feel and sometimes act like a kid around other adults.

Opposition: You became what psychologists call the "parentified child." You learned to parent your parents, by taking care of their emotional needs, not being a bother, and always making them proud.

Dynamic: You had perfectionistic parents.

Fusion: You developed a false and ideal presentation of who you are to avoid judgment and shame.

Opposition: You throw your values and standards to the wind and give up trying to be a good person, knowing you will never be good enough.

What did you identify with in this list? Was it a relief, as in "some lights went on"? Was it a negative experience, such as "This brings up old stuff I don't like to look at"? Did you identify with more than one pattern? Write down any insights you may have had. This will help you continue to understand your relational past so that the future is better for you.

Connecting your past to your present is an important part of moving beyond boundaries. When you identify your narrative—the situation that shaped your early relationships and life experiences—and understand your response to that narrative, you are well on your way to making sense of your past relational choices. This process is not a blame game, nor is it disloyal. It is an attempt to understand what is going on at a deeper level so you can grow, forgive, change, and heal. I strongly encourage you to spend some time connecting the dots between your past and your present. It takes work and often courage, but it is well worth the effort. In addition to providing personal insights that will help you grow, it will also help you to understand why you have had relational difficulties in the first place.

What's Your Missing Piece?

Let's suppose you have identified your family dynamic, either from one of the examples above or based on your own reflections. In what way does this affect your relational choices? Here's the answer: *unhealed relational wounds drive us to compulsive attempts to repair the damage.* That is, without being aware of it, we seek out people we believe can "fix" what's wrong with us or help us find a piece of ourselves we feel is missing. We function emotionally like the starving man who looks in a dumpster and sees lunch instead of garbage. His perception is so driven by his need that he is willing to eat something that might make him sick.

Though we may not be aware of it, something in us wants completeness. God has "set eternity in the human heart" (Ecclesiastes 3:11), and we long for him and the full life he promises. But if we remain unaware of the powerful forces at work within us—our family dynamic and how we responded to it—we will be blind to its influence and seek out the completeness we lack by making all the wrong choices. For example, consider the following scenarios:

- The overly nice person lacks assertiveness and the ability to confront, so he attracts controlling and aggressive people.

- The overly angry person can't allow herself to feel helpless or sad, so she finds empathic people who won't confront her moods.

- The rigid, black-and-white person is not able to let go of control, so he seeks out spontaneous, creative people who won't try to control him.

- The overresponsible, guilt-ridden person lacks self-care, so she finds self-absorbed people who care for no one but themselves.

- The person who can't connect or trust easily goes through life without love and attachment, so he finds a warm, caring person who is somewhat helpless and dependent.

Of course, the problem is that these kinds of responses do not reflect God's intentions for us. And they don't lead to healthy or fulfilling connections.

These missing pieces are part of what is called the internalization process. We become who we are by incorporating experiences that we have with other people. On a developmental level, kids come into this life incomplete. In the process of healthy development, they receive safety and acceptance and develop assertiveness, self-control, and self-care that prepare them for life on their own. Once internalization is complete, we become functioning adults who are called to pursue wholeness; or, in Jesus' words, "What I'm saying is, Grow up. You're kingdom subjects. Now live like it. Live out your God-created identity" (Matthew 5:48 MSG). What Jesus means is that he wants us to be mature and complete. But we are not complete. We have missing pieces—soul holes we carry from childhood into adulthood. The path to completeness or wholeness is to find a relational context—a healthy church, small group, mentor, or therapist—who can help us finish the emotional work that enables us to grow into the capacities we lack and become who we are meant to be.

This is especially important in romantic relationships, where there is often a glitch in our emotional hardware. We feel strongly that the other person will complete us, but not in the way I am describing. It is not about becoming more connected, intimate, assertive, or real. It is about being in the presence of someone else who has those attributes *without having to take responsibility to learn them.* "You complete me" is a great line from the movie *Jerry Maguire,* but it doesn't work in real relationships. You can't outsource health. You must learn it all and take it inside your skin. Complete people then attract other complete people. That is why most of us need to put less energy into romance and more into personal growth. It pays off later in romance.

Understanding your missing pieces also pays off in other ways. Perhaps your concern in reading this book isn't about a marriage or dating relationship. It may be that the difficult relationship you need to address is with your parents, siblings, or a person from your childhood. Or it's about a work relationship. Whatever your interest, you will find great benefit, in looking at the missing pieces, to understanding why things ended up like they did. The more information, the better for you.

Keep Searching to Connect the Dots

Some individuals struggle to recognize in their own lives the kind of patterns I have described here. As far as they can tell, there are no dots to connect. They either cannot identify harmful relational patterns, or if they can, they don't believe those patterns have affected them or have any influence or power over them. Perhaps you feel something similar.

Certainly it's possible that you picked the person you picked to love, marry, trust, or invest in and were simply fooled. That can happen. Sad to say, there are people whose insides are so dark that they are adroit at manipulating others' impressions of them. At the same time, however, we are talking about important and significant relationships. These aren't people you have coffee with once a month. These are people with whom you have spent a good deal of time. And character, for good or for bad, always emerges over time. It cannot be completely disguised over a lifetime of scrutiny, anymore than a financially dishonest organization can withstand an extended IRS audit. Reality always emerges over time.

If you're having difficulty connecting the dots, you may find it helpful to ask yourself this question: "Why did I trust so completely and so readily?" Often, when a person allows herself to become curious rather than defensive about this, she experiences a breakthrough. She is able to connect the dots to a family of origin in which, for example, it was inappropriate to ask tough questions, require responsibility, and confront things that didn't make sense. Then she can see how she allowed the wrong types of people to take advantage of her trusting nature. Go the extra step and allow yourself to be curious about this question. See what emerges.

The Past Must Become the Past

There are three periods of time: past, present, and future. Life goes best for us when we remember and learn from the past, when we engage fully in the present, and when we look forward to the future because we have handled the past and present in healthy ways. But when we fail to learn and heal from our past relational patterns, our past remains our present. We behave and react in ways that have more to do with fighting old battles and attempting to get someone to love us than they do with engaging legitimate needs in the present. We are stuck in a time warp, and our present is contaminated with old arguments, old hurts, and old relational dances that never resolve. We stay in an endless cycle that exhausts and discourages us.

There is no room for the past in the present. It must be placed where it belongs, in memory and in lessons learned. When you connect the dots between past and present, your relational future is much brighter.

8

You Grieve and Let It Go

A great deal of the music people listen to, especially country western music, is about love: love gained and love gone bad. Songs about cheating, mistreating, leaving. They give people something to identify with their experience and words to convey what they are feeling in a time of loss. The great majority of the love-gone-bad songs can be placed in one of two categories: *don't leave me* and *I'm moving on*. Don't-leave-me songs are full of pain and angst about how deeply the person wants to keep the one who is distancing himself or herself from the relationship and how that person promises to do whatever it takes to make the reconnection — *I'll be there for you, I'll change my ways*, etc. The moving-on songs are less emotional and more matter-of-fact: *You did me wrong, it's over, and I'm glad to be out of it. I'm moving on.*

Both types of love-gone-bad songs provide a necessary part of the picture. When something goes wrong in a relationship, it feels bad, and you want the problem to end. That's where the "don't leave me" part comes in. It's a way of persuading the person to reconcile or return. It also often has the effect of postponing the inevitable.

Ultimately, however, if the relationship is truly over, you must move on. Sometimes you move on to a life without romance or that particular friendship or family connection. Sometimes you move toward another new relationship. In some fortunate cases, people move to a restored and transformed relationship with the other person, if that individual is willing to change. One way or another, moving on is the way to go. But if you are going to truly let go of the past in a way that benefits you the most, you must do it the right way.

By themselves, neither the protest stance nor moving on is completely the right way; there is a missing piece. The piece that completes the picture — and is usually the most difficult — is what happens between protest and moving on, which is grief. Grief is what enables you to fully let go. It frees you, it clears your mind, and it helps heal the injuries. You must grieve what was. You must grieve it well and thoroughly before you are ready to go beyond boundaries into new intimacy.

Grief: What It Is and What It Does for You

Grief helps us process the reality of loss. Simply put, grief is *letting go of what you cannot keep*. Grief requires accepting, both mentally and emotionally, that something you loved and valued is no more. There are many areas of life in which we can experience loss and for which we need to grieve:

- The dissolution of a marriage
- The end of a dating relationship
- Family ties that break down

- Friendships that end
- The death of a loved one
- Career opportunities that don't materialize
- A relapse into addiction after years of sobriety
- Declining physical health
- Financial setbacks
- A trauma that forever mars an otherwise happy childhood

These represent important and life-changing experiences. However, just the fact that you have experienced losses doesn't mean you can't have a great and meaningful life. People endure great losses, like the ones mentioned earlier, and still have lives that are full and rich. The process of grieving losses is what helps you to deal with them and move on. This process is especially important when it comes to relational losses.

Grief helps you redirect your energies and focus on what you can have and what is good in your life. It provides a way to clear out regrets and hurts as a way to make room for the new. And *grief converts a wound into a memory.* That is, when you learn the process of letting go, the pain you feel in the present moves down your neurological pathways into your memory banks, where the past resides. In the memory banks, you can review the past, understand the past, and learn from the past.

Without grief, the wound never becomes a memory. You remain stuck in reexperiencing the hurt and hard times over and over again. Much like someone who suffers from post-traumatic stress disorder, people who fail to grieve experience a cycle of repeated thoughts and feelings, almost like

flashbacks, that offer no relief. Grief ends this cycle and reca-
librates your mind.

Six Components for Grieving a Lost Relationship

When it comes to the loss of a significant relationship, there
are six essential components necessary for grief to do its work.

1. Acknowledge the Attachment

We get attached to people. That is the draw. And without
an emotional attachment, there is nothing to grieve. This may
seem obvious, but it is important to state it. *The greater the
grief you feel, the greater the love you have for the person
you lost.* And you can't instantly undo the attachment. In the
context of a relationship, you can't simply stop feeling your
feelings for someone just because the relationship is severed
or changes. As we've noted before, the pain you feel is a good
thing; it is a sign that you are alive inside.

2. Accept That You Can't Control the Loss

Grief requires that you give up control of the other person's
decision and admit that you do not have the power to make
him or her love you or move toward you. You are accepting
a type of helplessness: "focused" helplessness, not the global
helplessness of the victim position. It's focused because you
can choose to let go, choose to let your feelings out, choose
to let other people in, and choose to even tell the person you
don't want the relationship to end. But in the end, you must
accept that the other person is in the driver's seat of his or her
own life and path, toward you or away from you. You are,

in that specific arena of life, helpless, because you don't have permission or power to change the other person's decisions.

This is a difficult area for most of us. No one wants to feel helpless. It renders us vulnerable and unable to make things happen the way we would like them to. I recently spoke with a woman on our radio program who described how her ex-husband had called her every day for the past four years—*after the marriage had ended*. He was unable to accept that the marriage was over. Some people think if they have one more talk with the other person and say the right thing at the right time, they can undo the alienation. Others think that if they become more lovable and attractive, that will work. The extreme cases engage in stalking behaviors. All of these behaviors are driven by a failure to accept the reality that one cannot control the loss of a relationship.

We resist helplessness when we don't want to lose love. However, the sooner you can allow yourself to experience focused helplessness—to admit that you have no control over the other person's decisions—the better off you will be.

Jesus allowed himself to experience focused helplessness by restraining his own power to make us love him: "Jerusalem, Jerusalem, you who kill the prophets and stone those sent to you, how often I have longed to gather your children together, as a hen gathers her chicks under her wings, and you were not willing" (Matthew 23:37). It is a model for us: if the All-Powerful could restrain his might to let people go, we who are finite in power can do the same.

3. Name What You Valued

When you value someone, you affirm that he or she is important to you. When the connection is over, there are certain aspects of the person and the relationship that you miss the most. These are the values you have to grieve. Here are some examples:

- *Warmth:* he was accessible and moved toward you
- *Vulnerability:* she allowed her weaknesses and insecurities to emerge
- *Structure:* she could focus and get things done
- *Intellect:* he was smart and interesting to talk to
- *Honesty:* he could hear and tell the truth
- *Spiritual values:* she loved God and helped you become closer to God
- *Acceptance:* she could care about you even with your failings and imperfections
- *Personal values:* he had similar values about love, family, and relationship
- *Culture:* your backgrounds meshed well

Sometimes, the value you need to grieve is connected to specific memories as well. It could be a trip you took or a private joke you shared. It might be a time of deep intimacy in which you were very close. Perhaps it was good times with the family.

Why is it important to name the specific things you valued? Because *you must say good-bye to the entire person, not simply the negative parts of the person.* You cannot walk away from the things you disliked, which may be the things that ended the relationship, without also saying good-bye to the things you loved as well. A half grief is never a healing grief.

Here's another way to think about it. Chances are you've

been in a situation in which a friend is sad about a relational loss, and you want to help. So you do the most instinctual and protective thing, which is to trash the other person! You might say things like, "I never knew what you saw in him." "You are better off without him." "He doesn't deserve you." Such statements are well-meaning and probably encourage your friend for awhile. But it also distances her from what she needs to say good-bye to, which is what she valued.

Moreover, it sets her back. The ungrieved "good parts" stay inside her mind and heart and haunt her. That is why some people can't get over a past relationship or why they find other people who aren't so good for them but remind them of what they missed. It is better to help your friend say things like, "I know he was controlling, but I do miss the good times." In that way, she is able to begin letting go of the whole person.

You need that as well. When your friends trash your ex, instead of feeling like a righteous victim, tell them, "I know she was all that, but I have been missing the good things, and I need you to let me talk about those too." It might feel a little humiliating—how can you be so weak that you still have feelings for a person who mistreated you? Go ahead and push through the humiliation. It just means you were attached to someone with both strengths and weaknesses. And you are valuing the good so that you can say a complete farewell.

4. Surround Yourself with People Who Are Comforting

Grief is letting go of something we can't keep, but nature abhors a vacuum. It is hard to let go of a relationship all by yourself, because there is a vacuum inside where the person used to be. In other words, you will continue reaching out and desiring the other person even though you know the relationship is over. Having people around you who have the capacity to comfort can help to fill the vacuum.

The process of comfort begins with God, "who comforts us in all our troubles, so that we can comfort those in any trouble with the comfort we ourselves receive from God" (2 Corinthians 1:4). How do you know if someone has the capacity to comfort? By the degree to which they remain present with you when you grieve. Being present means they don't try to give you advice, cheer you up, or change the topic. That's what people who are anxious about their own losses do. But people who are familiar with loss know how to just be with you. They give you eye contact, are sometimes quiet, and sometimes are just empathic. Allowing yourself to be comforted by others not only salves your grief, it also greatly reduces the power of the vacuum.

You may have little experience with grief and letting go. I find that many businesspeople, for example, will simply move on from a bad situation or relationship without feeling their sadness. It is important, however, to be intentional about grief and not skip over it. Otherwise, you run the risk of never being able to fully let go of a person or lost opportunity in your past.

5. *Allow the Sadness*

The emotion of sadness encompasses both longing and mourning. When you are sad, your heart feels downcast. Tears may come. Even though you may have to wait for these emotions to come—you can't manufacture them at will—there are things you can do that will help you access your sadness.

- Intentionally set aside time to step away from your busy routines and activities and settle into a quiet place.
  - Think about the person you lost.
  - Recall the negative aspects of the relationship, but don't allow yourself to stay angry or to get sidetracked by an internal argument about how wrong it was.
  - Remember the good aspects of the relationship and the warm times.
- Meet with a friend or counselor and tell him about the things you remember and your experiences with the other person.
- Ask a friend to play the part of your difficult person in a role-play conversation, in which you say what needs to be said: "I care about you, and even though it's been hard, I always will. Good-bye." If you are going to talk to the person, this will help you experience the feelings and fears ahead of time. If you don't have the opportunity to talk to the person, the role-play can still help you work through what you feel and resolve it.

Some combination of activities like these can help you get out of the *doing* mode and into the *feeling* mode. Then you will more readily access the sad emotions that must come. By welcoming your sadness, you allow your feelings to simply catch up with and ally with your thoughts about the reality of the loss.[4]

6. *Give Yourself the Gift of Time*

Time is like an oven. It takes all the raw ingredients of grief and loss that we've talked about so far and cooks them up into something new; it transforms them, creating a new way for you to experience your loss. You cannot microwave grief. However, you can speed up the process by taking time and devoting energy to working through this process. Alternatively, you can also prolong your grief, sometimes forever. You don't want that for yourself. You want to get it done right so that you can move on.

I once worked with a couple whose adult son, Brian, was a drug addict. He had rejected their help and the relationship they wanted to have with him. He was determined to go his own way and saw no reason to involve them in his life.

Brian's father mourned the loss of his son over a period of several months and eventually began to invest his energies into other pursuits and family relationships. Brian's mother, however, hated the idea of sadness—it was uncomfortable, and she did not like the sense of being out of control. So she would allow herself to feel a little sadness and then go through periods of "getting herself together." She would tell me, "I'm done with this grief stuff. I have accepted that Brian doesn't want us in his life. That's his choice, he's a grown-up. It's time to move on." And every time, within a few weeks she became lethargic, had trouble concentrating, and felt weepy about her son. Then she would be a little bit sad again, followed by another round of being "done with it" again.

I felt bad for her. She had come from a professional family in which sadness was seen as a weakness, so the feelings caused a great deal of shame and self-condemnation within her. I told her, "Maybe you're done, but I doubt it. This is the fourth time you have struggled with your sad feelings like this." Then I turned to her husband and said, "Why don't you tell her how you feel about her sad feelings about Brian?" He looked at her and said, "You're the only other person in the world who understands what we are going through. When you allow yourself to feel our sadness, it brings me closer to you and I feel hope for us." When she heard that, she began to soften. She was able to stay with her sadness and slowly did make steady progress—instead of the false starts and stops —in letting Brian go.

While some people such as Brian's mom resist their grief, others can get frozen in a permanent state of grief. They access their sadness, but something breaks down, and they cannot move on. So they continue years of living in loss and have difficulty being happy. Sometimes the breakdown is due to isolation and not having enough safe people with whom to process their loss. Sometimes it is because they idealize the person they lost and can't imagine anyone could replace them; they build a mental shrine to that person. People whose spouses or parents have died often suffer from this. Making another attachment seems disloyal to the other person's memory, so they sacrifice their opportunities for a good life in the future on the altar of the life they can no longer have.

If you think you may be frozen in this way, it will help to make a list of the positive and negative qualities of the person and reflect on them. This is not dishonoring to the individual. It is simply a way to allow you to say good-bye to the real person, so that you don't stay stuck in seeing only the good parts.

These six components have an order and a structure to them. They work. But remember that grief has its own pace as well. One part may take more or less time than you expected. Don't attempt to force or control your grief process. Give yourself margin within the components. In time, you will be able to let go of the relationship and move on.

Grieving a Living Person

Letting go of a relationship when the individual has passed away is no easy task. However, it can be even harder in some ways when the person is still alive. This was the case with Brian, whose parents had to grieve the loss of their relationship with him. As the saying goes, where there is life, there is hope, and if you know the person is still breathing, it is easy to imagine scenarios, conversations, and tactics that could return and restore the relationship. We all have hope somewhere inside us, the anticipation of a future good. We need hope, because it helps us endure a difficult present, knowing that the future will be an improvement. However, when that capacity for hope attaches to a person simply because he or she is alive—not for any sound reason that makes sense—it is a vain hope.

If this is your situation, you don't want to waste any more time on vain hope. The only thing it does is slow down your ability to move beyond boundaries and into great relationships. You may need to focus on this issue. Here are a few ideas that might help:

- Tell yourself that you still have a death to deal with: the person is not dead, but the relationship is.

- Write down the evidence you have of the loss and reflect on it: the divorce paper, the person has another relationship, there is no change in the person's toxicity.

- Ask a friend to tell you why he or she thinks the relationship is over and listen to it from his or her perspective.

Giving up vain hope doesn't mean that relational miracles don't occur. I have seen many dead connections resurrected. So be open to the possibility. But let go. You can enter sadness and still leave a door open at the same time. It sounds like it can't be done, but it can in this way: you are putting your energy and focus into the next steps and the next relationships. But you are not God, and if God miraculously changes the situation, you can respond to that. Move ahead, but let God be God.

But what do you do if the relationship is not over? For example, say you are married, and it is a hard marriage, but you want to keep the commitment and repair whatever is broken, even though it is painful. Is this a matter of grief? Yes, it still is. It is not about letting go and saying good-bye to the person or the relationship; they are still in the picture. But you do have a loss: *the loss of the good that was there.*

There were good days and times of connection and happiness before things began to go wrong. It may sound strange to grieve the lost, good parts of your relationship and still relate to or even live with the person, but the idea still holds: you have suffered a loss, and it must be grieved. Don't prevent yourself from grieving just because you are still in the relationship. The loss is still real and important to you.

If the relationship never had a good season, how do you grieve that? For whatever reason, character issues, disconnection, control, manipulations, addictions, and even abuse could have been the norm from the beginning of the relationship. Obviously, you can't grieve that—there is nothing in the relationship to grieve. That is, except for one thing: *the hope.* That is, the hope of what you wanted to happen. You grieve your dreams and desires for love, connection, success, partnership, acceptance, or support.

We generally begin a friendship, a family relationship, a business relationship, or a courtship with some sort of hope of a good outcome. Why else would we try to connect in the first place? If you are in a situation in which you feel there is nothing good about the relationship to grieve, you can grieve your lost hopes and what did not happen. Again, I need to say that I have seen relationships that were stillborn and never fulfilling that, with work, began to thrive in health and intimacy. So if the structure of the relationship still exists, I encourage you to continue working for a better future, while at the same time saying good-bye to your dreams of the past.

You Have Nothing to Fear from Grief

Allow me to add a bit of perspective here, especially if concentrating on grief and understanding its nature are new to you. Grief doesn't have to control or consume your life. Depending on the situation, it can take days or it can take years. How long it takes all depends on how important the relationship was to you, whom you choose to help you along, and how focused you are in the process. But don't be afraid of your grief. You can have a good life and still let go of that which is no longer yours. Take it from wise King Solomon, "A sad face is good for the heart" (Ecclesiastes 7:3).

Grief is like the weather; it's always changing and often unpredictable. It is more organic than systematic. So while you are in the season of letting go of the relationship or a part of the relationship, allow yourself to engage in it and embrace it. Your grief will subside, and you can regain joy and positive feelings. Then another wave of grief will likely return. But the process works in such a way that each time you engage in grief, the bottom—the lowest part of the sadness—should be a little less severe and a little less dark. And in time, you will be yourself, actually more than yourself—because you have integrated and metabolized the loss of the relationship and learned from it.

9

You Develop
Growth Friendships

There is unlocked and untapped potential in most friendships. There is the potential to learn something from the other person's different life experiences. The potential to be open and real with someone in a new way. The potential to see yourself in a fresh way through another's perspective on you. Developing the untapped potential in your friendships is a good thing for your life all by itself, but it has the added benefit of also helping you prepare yourself for the risks and vulnerabilities you want to take in a future relationship. Developing a new way to look at and maximize your friendships is an essential step in preparing yourself to move beyond boundaries.

The Right Friendships Can Meet the Need

Let's return to your difficult relationship. The fact that this person occupies so much space in your mind and heart means she was significant to you; she mattered. In fact, she probably met some important need you have or at least something you wanted to happen. It might have been unconditional love, understanding, respect, or dependability, for example.

There is nothing wrong with having these needs; God designed you that way. Just as you and I need vitamins and minerals from our food, we need support and care from others. This is true whether the context is romance, family, friendship, or work. It is how we survive, grow, and succeed in life. People — relationships — are the delivery system of God's provision for his children: we are "good stewards of the manifold grace of God" (1 Peter 4:10 KJV).[5]

However, when things go wrong in a relationship and they *stay wrong*, it can be that the other person is trying to send you a message. The message goes something like this: *I am disqualifying myself from meeting your need*. That is, I am either unable or unwilling to provide the love, understanding, respect, or dependability you require. It may be a matter of her own brokenness, her lack of investment in you, some way she sees you in a negative light, or her own self-absorption. Whatever the reason, she removes the ingredient from you. This poses a problem. Your need doesn't go away when the relationship does. It does not vanish. It still exists. You still must have that need met. But your need is not for *her*; your need is for something she possesses and has made unavailable.

This is an important distinction to make. When people encounter a tough relationship, they can usually acknowledge the value of grief, as we presented in the last chapter, and work on letting go. Grief makes sense to them and helps them move on. But they are not always as aware that they have another need — beyond their need for the relationship — and that they must look elsewhere to meet it.

This is where the friendship piece of the equation comes in. It is about replacement. You cannot replace your difficult person with an exact replica of that person. *But,* for you to be ready to risk again, *you must replace the need that person met in your life.*

People are dispensable. That may sound harsh, so let me explain. We are all unique and precious to God, but we are not indispensable. If my wife and I die before our kids are out on their own, they would be in a position of need. They would still need some sort of parenting, not being ready to meet the demands of life. They would need help in finishing school, becoming ready for adult relationships, learning how to find and keep a job, handling finances, becoming spiritually mature, and so forth. Those needs would still be there, residing within the kids.

That is why we set our children up with godparents. If anything happens, these people, along with other supportive individuals, would help with that finishing-up work. No one could "be" the original mom and dad. But others could provide the elements the kids need. That's what I mean when I say people are dispensable—it's possible for others to take up their roles and tasks.

What did you need from your broken relationship? There are probably a few things that come to mind. One of your most important next steps is to develop the untapped potential in your friendships by allowing the good people who care about you to help you meet those needs. If what you needed from the broken relationship was empathy, make sure your friends are able to be empathetic, to feel your feelings with you. If you needed safety, choose friends who are without an ounce of condemnation or judgment. If it was wisdom, you need friends who are skilled in living and making good decisions. Think beyond your needs for the person you lost and focus on the roles he or she played in your life and the specific needs that were met.

Here is why this is so important as you prepare to find a new relationship or reenter the old one. *You must move from need to desire.* You must fill your emotional tank. That is, you cannot be in a position of deprivation and emptiness when you take a relational risk. It sets you up for more problems and places you in jeopardy. If you are still in a state of need, that need can drive you to unsafe relationships, to allowing someone else to control you and to becoming dependent in a way that can hurt you. If, however, you have let others in and you are "rooted and established in love" (Ephesians 3:17), you are operating from a solid foundation, and your needs have already been met. You are much less vulnerable to being injured or set back.

Tony, a businessman I coached, had a company that he co-owned with a partner. He had a great deal of respect for the partner, who was older and had more experience in the field. As time went on, however, the partner began to take more control of the business than was right or fair. He cut deals on the side that benefited him alone. He used questionable reasons to justify paying himself more than his partner.

It wasn't long until Tony and his partner began having conflicts about these things. The elder partner had a strong streak of entitlement; that is, he thought he deserved more than he actually did. The conflict wasn't resolved, the partnership ended, and the two split up. This was a terrible time for Tony. He genuinely cared for his former partner and not only missed him as a person, but also missed the guidance and wisdom he had received from him.

As he began scouting the horizon for his next professional step, I could see that he tended to give too much power and authority to older, mature men. The fact that his own father had not been involved in his childhood was no surprise. But I was concerned that he had a vulnerability that needed to be addressed. I was afraid he would strike up another partnership with the wrong person and repeat the nightmare.

I recommended that he try working on his own for a while and become involved with a few successful businesspeople just as friends. He found some, and they became more than friends. They became confidants. They were trustworthy people who also had a great deal of business acumen. This was a period of rapid personal and professional growth for this man. He became more confident in his own abilities and ultimately found another business partner. This time, he chose someone who was more of an equal rather than a father figure or mentor. He was not desperate for the needs the former partner had met.

Do the detective work on yourself. Identify your needs and replace the person. God is a God of replacement, not of emptiness and deprivation: "I will repay you for the years the locusts have eaten" (Joel 2:25). He knows that in order to become the people he wants us to be, we must find the emotional vitamins and minerals we have been denied.

Distinguish between Maintenance Needs and Healing Needs

There is a growth step beyond replacement, however. Ultimately, it has to do with you growing stronger and more complete as a person. The growth step is this: *there are some needs that, at some point, must be met and resolved, and you must begin to take over the jobs for yourself.* The growth step is this: *what others have done for you, you will often now be able to do for yourself.* By this, I do not mean replacing or leaving the relationships. I would hope you keep the good ones for many years. I am referring to your own growth and maturity. Here is what I mean.

Relationships were designed to provide you with things you need to grow and to thrive—grace, acceptance, structure, advice, and encouragement. But you live in two time zones, so to speak. You live in the present, in which your closer friends provide you with these elements of growth. And you live in the past, where there are injuries and unhealed issues. These old wounds may have diminished your ability to trust or say no, for example. In order to heal from past injuries, you need the elements relationships provide not for maintenance-level growth—the everyday support we all need—but for healing. For example, even the healthiest and most robust plant needs water, sun, and soil on a regular basis in order to survive and grow. But a sick plant needs more care, more attention, and even special nutrients in order to heal what ails.

That is what happened to the young businessman whose story I shared earlier. He continued to internalize and receive the support, wisdom, and mentoring of other men. Over time, he not only worked through the needs he had for his previous partner's acumen, he grew professionally himself and gradually became an equal with his friends. His maturity process and his hard work increased his strengths and healed his injuries. The result was that his relational connections have continued, but less on a helping level than a mutual give-and-take level. He provides support and perspective to the same people who, during his tough time, did all the providing for him.

What does this mean for you? It means that you need to distinguish between your relational maintenance needs and your relational healing needs. Then you can determine the needs your friends are meeting or whether you need to seek out some new relationships to help you with needs that aren't being met.

For example, we all need connection; this is a basic relational maintenance need. You need some significant supportive and accepting conversations several times a week from the right people, and there is no expiration date on that; it is forever. However, when you have a broken relationship, this is a repair need. It means that deep within you, there is isolation and aloneness. If you lack the ability to reach out and let someone in—and feel good about doing so—your feelings of isolation won't go away even if you are surrounded by people who care for you. For some people, this can mean they always feel needy and dependent, no matter how much support they receive. It's like trying to fill up a tire with a slow leak. No matter how much support is pumped into such people, they never feel as if their needs are met. Others may feel detached and disconnected rather than needy. They want to connect, but they have difficulty letting people in.

Relational injuries like these require special care, generally beyond what normal supportive relationships deliver: a small group that can go deep and is dedicated to repairing connection problems or a good therapist, for example. Then, when the relational injury is brought out and processed, the person can lean into friendships for healing needs for a season before moving on to a maintenance level of relationships. Relational maintenance needs and healing needs may feel as though they are the same thing; both involve the emotion of loneliness or of deep isolation. But they are very different in their nature and must not be treated the same way.

Let's Talk about Love

Romance is a great gift from God and can be the source of much happiness and joy. At its best, it is a wonderful enhancement to the intimacy between a man and a woman. Used the wrong way, however, it can hamper your growth toward vulnerability and intimacy. Romance can muddy the waters in your growth and relationships. Think of it this way: *while the best romantic relationships are also friendships, most friendships can't be romantic.* Yet some people struggle with a tendency to see romance as the highest and most special form of relationship. They may appreciate their friends, but life really comes alive when they are falling in love.

No doubt about it, romantic love does have an energy to it that is like no other: passion, dreams, sexuality, and desires for deep closeness all emerge in a highly emotional way. The problem comes when romance is seen as the ultimate relational experience, superior to other types. Hollywood movies readily convey this idea. A person has good friendships, a successful career, and fun hobbies. But there is an emptiness that only the lack of romantic love would fulfill. It sometimes comes across as if the character's whole life is on hold until the right person comes along, and then life has meaning. When this is the case, it means that *friends are not allowed into the deeper places where the romantic relationship resides.* When we fail to allow our friendships access to the deeper places in our hearts, we often experience emptiness and longing until romance comes along.

Relationally speaking, this puts the cart before the horse. The reality is that a person with a good and whole life, who is happy without romance, actually stands a much better chance of having a great romance if she finds that special someone. And the reverse is equally true. The person who is romantically vulnerable and places too much emphasis on romance is more likely, over time, to struggle when she falls in love. Without the foundation of great friends and character maturity, romance tends to disintegrate. I have counseled too many couples who didn't understand that romance comes after growth and friendships; in order to rebuild, they had a great deal of demolition work to do on their relationship.

Is there a loss when you live without romance? Yes. It can be especially painful if you have been in love and grieve the loss of this wonderful arena of life. If you want to fall in love, there is a lot right and nothing wrong in actively looking for the right person to fall in love with. But, if for whatever reason romance is no longer in the picture, it's important to know that Hollywood is wrong. Your life can be full, meaningful, fun, and productive without romance—and I know many people who feel that way. They are active in their faith, their friendships, and their careers, and they would say they aren't missing anything.

Perhaps part of the problem is that it's hard to wrap our minds around an absence—a negative—and feel good about it. Think about it: She is single. They are childless. He lost his career. Their relationship broke up. These are all negatives, some more significant than others. But the point is, *the existence of a negative is just part of the story*. Get the whole picture.

She is single and dedicates a lot of time to activities, relationships, and causes she enjoys. As a childless couple, they have become the favorite aunt and uncle to lots of nieces and nephews. He lost his career and during the process of recalibrating his life reclaimed relationships and deeper values he had been missing. Their relationship broke up, and he has learned a great deal about himself through the process. The romantic ideal allows little room for loss, in the same way that children's stories must have a happy ending. But in adult life, much happiness can come because of and in spite of losses.

If you think you might have a romantic vulnerability, it's a good idea to check out how much mental and emotional energy you invest into the opposite sex. Do most of your conversations with your friends revolve around how your dating life or marriage is doing? Or is there a balance between romance, friendship, family, career, personal life, activities, and spiritual life? Look at your calendar. Do you find yourself kidnapped by love and spending less time with your friends when you're in a dating relationship? You may be surprised at what happens if others can enter that part of life where only romance was permitted.

There are two ways to recalibrate this so that you are more in balance when you have a romantic vulnerability. The first is to become active and positive and do what active, positive people do: they fill up their schedules with meaningful people and activities that matter to them. So don't keep calendar space open just in case you fall in love or so you can miss romance. There is a life out there to enjoy, engage in, and feel connected to and productive. This will help.

The second way is a bit more interior, but just as important. It is to enter the grief process and let go of whatever caused you to go after romance when you needed love. This is such a common problem. A successful and intelligent single person will find herself overly involved in romantic relationships. When she does some psychological digging, she will often find out that she had a significant relationship who was distant and unavailable. It could be a parent, for example. So, since she could not get connected in the normal way of having attention, understanding, interest, and empathy, she diverted her need into the romantic sphere. Normal longings for love and support become longings for romantic, passionate love. And it always backfires.

If this is your situation, it will help for you to allow your sad feelings about having had to divert yourself that way to be expressed and comforted. Grief will help you move on and learn to feel the value in nonromantic, healthy relationships. Let the old way of getting connected go, keep romance in its proper perspective, and you will be better for it.

Conclusion

Remember the cover of this book. There is an opening in the wall, where relationship can come in and out, in a safe way. Good, growth-producing friendships should be the first ones who enter that space. They will pave the way for more risky relationships.

Pointers

If you have determined that you might have a romantic vulnerability, admit that to your safe people and tell them you want to learn how to be connected to them at the same level that you previously reserved for romance alone. Or, if you are dating or married, take some risks with your safe people and let them know your emotional side. You will find that you have more to offer in your romantic relationship and that you are also clearer about yourself, as the tank is full.

Close friendships, small groups, mentors, spiritual directors, coaches, and counselors all form part of the growth plan for you. Pay attention to these people. Be intentional about spending time with them. They are not a way to pass the time between marriages or love interests. They are at the center of your life.

As I was working on this book, I hit a perfect storm of this writing, another project, and some unexpected business travel. Things got very busy, and I ended up writing on a Saturday night into the wee hours of Sunday morning. The growth group that my wife and I belong to meets on Sunday mornings. Barbi said, "You've had very little sleep, do you want to sleep in?" I thought about it. I really didn't feel any obligation to go, as everyone would understand and be supportive. But I was aware that I just didn't want to miss being with them. So we went. I was dragging, but I get a lot personally from the group, so it was worth it. Find your own team. Get involved. Get connected to the life that is there.

10

You Trust Your Defining Boundaries

It's time for a quick review. You have two types of boundaries: *defining boundaries* that identify who you are as a person and *protective boundaries* that keep you safe in unsafe situations. You must never give up your defining boundaries. But sooner or later, when you are around the right new relationship or an improved present relationship, you will have to give up your protective boundaries.

It takes energy, intentionality, and time to develop either kind of boundary. I can't tell you how many people over the years have told me, "I read the original *Boundaries* book, and it took me a long, long time to make changes." Establishing boundaries requires identifying the relational problem, securing support and safe relationships, naming what is wrong and what must change, creating consequences if there is no response, having the conversation or conversations with the person, and following through. Boundaries are much more than "Just say no."

Establishing protective boundaries can be especially

demanding. It's a little like always holding your breath. You have to stay somewhat vigilant and careful to make sure you're following the plan and not enabling the other person or allowing him to manipulate you. Sooner or later, you want to stop holding your breath and just relax.

Because establishing boundaries requires so much time and effort, there is also some work involved in moving beyond boundaries. And when you begin to take those first steps, it is especially important to make clear distinctions between defining and protective boundaries. We tend to generalize or globalize our experiences. So, if I am careful with a parent, spouse, or whomever, I may find it difficult to refrain from being careful when I'm with people who are not safe.

It's a little like the response of a soldier, now back home, who ducks for cover when he hears a car backfire. His jarring experiences in combat prompt him to react to the sound as if he's been shot at even though he's no longer in a war zone. Similarly, it can be difficult to let down your guard after working so hard to keep it up. You are still in protection mode.

The big picture is this: *the healthier your defining boundaries are, the less you will need your protective boundaries.* The more clear you are about who you are and what is important to you, the less you will need to be self-protective. That doesn't mean you will never have to guard your heart. That is part of life. But you will be more confident in your choices and in your relationships. You will be able to be vulnerable with the right people, and you will attract fewer controlling people as well.

It's Time to Stretch and Develop Your Defining Boundaries

As you prepare to move ahead into a more open and vulnerable existence, you need to pay more attention to your defining boundaries and to living without your protective boundaries. Let's look at some practical ways you can stretch and develop your defining boundaries.

Agree without Fear of Being Compliant or Controlled

Often, people who have established boundaries have done so because they feel they were the world's worst doormat. They said what others wanted them to say, they went along with what others wanted, and they found themselves feeling drained and powerless. When they start saying no, and it works well, they finally have more self-control, freedom, and a sense of empowerment to make their own choices.

However, they sometimes develop a knee-jerk "no" response. They are concerned that they may not be strong enough to hold on to their feelings and identity, so they say "no" to everything and everyone *simply to preserve their autonomy*. This is what psychologists call oppositionalism. Having lived under the control of others for so long, they worry that if they agree, say yes, or go along with someone, they will lose all self-definition, undo all the work they have done, and slide downhill into being a doormat again. That is unacceptable to them—and it should be.

I worked with a couple where the husband was controlling, and the wife was losing herself in the marriage. They did a lot of good work. He began to give up the control, she started speaking up, and they drew closer. But after a while, I noticed that she disagreed with whatever he said about anything—

the relationship, the kids, politics, or even the weather. She always had an opposing viewpoint. So I said to her, "You don't need this anymore." To her credit, she understood and agreed. She was learning to trust her husband and to trust herself, so she just needed a reminder.

Here is the point: people who feel secure can agree with someone else and still be separate from and equal to them. Learn to trust the reality that you can let your yes be yes and your no be no, and that you have not lost anything. If you do find you are becoming a doormat again, it may be time to concentrate on your fear: *Am I intimidated by another person? Am I trying to avoid their negative reaction? How can I hold on to myself, and care about them, without giving in to fears that they will not respond well?* Realize that most of our fears are not catastrophes, and in those cases when you have reason to be afraid, get relational support. That clears up most of the problem pretty quickly.

Normalize Truthfulness

You do have opinions, feelings, values, and thoughts that are yours, right? Actually, if you are reading this book, it is proof you do, because something in you decided that you wanted to learn more about the topic. One of the most helpful things you can do to strengthen your defining boundaries is to make truthfulness a normal and expected part of your life. That is, it's not enough to simply love and care for others. You must also be a person who brings truth and reality into your relationships. Truthfulness should not be the exception, it should be the norm.

I was riding to a business meeting with some friends the other day, and the woman driving wasn't sure about how to get where we were going. The other man in the car and I were talking and not paying attention to her driving. Finally, she interrupted us and said, "I need some help with the directions." She wasn't bugged or emotional at all. She didn't wait for a conversational lapse before saying something, either. She was just being truthful about the fact that she needed our help with the directions. This is living with truth as the norm.

Your opinions and feelings are part of who you are; they are your truth. Some are "actual truth"; that is, they represent verifiable and objective reality. Some are your own experiences and perceptions. They may not be "actual truth," but they are your own subjective truth. Subjective truth must ultimately bend its knee to actual truth, but that does not mean subjective truth is unimportant. For example, I once served on an organizational committee with a man named Jason. Jason tended to avoid making eye contact. He made good contributions to the committee, but he tended to look away when he spoke. I felt a little uneasy around him and thought he might not be a trustworthy person.

I said to one of the other members who knew him well, "I'm an eye-contact person, and Jason seems to avoid it. Is he a stand-up person?"

"You have no idea how stand-up he is," the other member said. "You can take what he says to the bank. Don't worry about the eye contact."

Over time, I found that this was true about Jason. In that case, actual truth differed from my subjective truth and trumped it. But the point is for you to be able to bring both kinds of truth into your life and relationships.

Normalizing truth means you make saying what is true and stating your opinion a routine part of your relationships. One of the saddest things in the relational world is to see someone who nods his head approvingly and looks interested in what is not interesting and agrees with what is not agreeable. Ironically, this makes overly compliant people—who very much want to be known and trusted—difficult people to know and trust. How do you trust someone who can't seem to come up with his own opinion? How do you know what his motive is for being agreeable? Is he protecting himself? Trying to get on your good side? Saying what sounds good because he's not sure what he thinks?

This is why people who have a hard time clarifying their own boundaries also often feel very alone. Their overcompliance keeps people from sensing who they really are, which means there is little actual and deep contact. When a person has that habit, it is generally a sign that she is afraid of her own definition and identity or that if the person she really is emerges, she will be met with criticism or judgment.

You must begin to trust that there is a real "you" who has some edges and is lovable. God loves honesty: "he delights in people who are trustworthy" (Proverbs 12:22b). And healthy people love honesty. Normalizing truthfulness in your relationships is simply inserting your own realities into the conversation, the meeting, or the event. It doesn't mean that you are being self-absorbed, rigidly opinionated, or controlling.

I have a friend who doesn't define himself well. He checks out the relational climate—other people's opinions—before venturing his own opinion. One night we were planning to go to dinner, and I asked him what kind of food he wanted. "Well, what do you like?" he asked. Normally, that kind of question is okay with me, but this wasn't the first time he'd worked the conversation this way, so I decided to push the envelope a little.

"I always go first here," I said, "C'mon, what do you really want?"

"I don't care, whatever you want," he said.

"Are you sure about that?"

"Sure, I'm sure."

"I was thinking that a fast-food drive-through dinner sounds good."

Nothing wrong with that, but I was not in the mood for it and figured neither was he. He laughed and said, "Oh yeah, sure," as if I were joking. I was serious and started driving to a fast-food place.

"Are you kidding?" he asked, looking incredulous.

"No," I said, "if you don't have an opinion, that's where we're going."

"Actually, I feel like Chinese tonight."

"Glad to hear it," I said, and turned the car around. Then I made sure he knew I thought it was great that he put out an opinion.

Now that's a lighthearted story, but it makes a point. Perhaps you're not as afraid as my friend is to define yourself, but you may be close. Instead of waiting to see if the coast is clear, get in the habit of saying what you observe, think, like, or don't like. People may agree or not agree. You may end up with fast food for dinner. But as you normalize truth telling in your relationships, you will find it easier to trust that your defining boundaries are good and that they will help you connect to others in healthy ways.

Let Someone Else Be Wrong

Sometimes your own experience, or subjective truth, does not fit with the experience or perceptions of another person.

People see things differently. Sometimes it's possible to identify that one person is mistaken and one is right; for example, if there is a disagreement about how much money is in the checking account, a bank statement provides an objective way to know who's right. Other times, it is just a matter of perspective and opinion; for example, which college football team has the most potential or what is the best way to discipline a child. Good friends are comfortable with these sorts of differences, even to the point of vigorous debate. One of my favorite things is for my wife and I to have dinner with interesting people who don't see the world as we do and get to know their worlds and opinions. It would be a pretty empty life to just hang out with carbon copies of each other.

However, when there is a significant disagreement on something you and the other person both feel strongly about, you may find yourself going on and on about it, returning to the topic, thinking of different ways to make your point, and in general making it difficult for everyone around you. There are certainly times for this: confronting someone on a major problem or sin or having an intervention for drug use, embezzlement, or infidelity, for example.

But after a few rounds of conversation, when both of you get to the point of digging in your heels, it's probably time to move on. Agree to disagree. Stop spending endless energy attempting to make the other person see it your way. If you find that you can't let go of the issue, it could mean you don't sufficiently trust your own defining boundaries. You might think something like this: *If I let him have the last word, I have given him control.* It is a fear that the other person's separate identity and definition are a threat to yours.

Give it up. Let him disagree, even if you are convinced beyond a shadow of a doubt that he is wrong. After a couple of attempts to make a point, just let it go. Letting it go is not an attempt to make the conversation more pleasant; it's a way of proving to yourself that you trust and feel secure in your own defining boundaries. Now, when you sit across the table from someone who does not see things your way and you have given up trying to make him see your reality, you are also stretching yourself. You are increasing your ability to be defined without having to prove anything. It brings you in touch with your anxiety to have people agree, your anxiety to have people see things your way, and your anxiety about the space between two people. And if you can become increasingly comfortable with that—especially with your anxieties about the space between two people—you will be able to connect more deeply and express yourself more honestly, all from a foundation of security in your own defining boundaries.

I was having an email exchange with a friend named Rob, and I sent him some information about a business project. Several days later, he asked, "Where's the info about the project?"

"I sent it a week ago," I said.

"No you didn't," Rob quickly replied.

I have a relational ground rule that when someone abruptly says, "That's not true," or "No, you didn't," I push once and let it go. Such a knee-jerk response generally means the person is reacting without much thought, so there's little room for dialogue.

I obeyed my ground rule and said, "I am pretty sure I sent it; did it not show up in your inbox?"

"I checked my inbox and my spam filter, and you didn't send it," Rob said.

My next response could have been something defensive

like, "How do you know whether or not I sent it? You weren't looking over my shoulder when I typed it." But this time, I just looked at him and said, "Okay, I'll resend it." I didn't want to get in a power struggle over something that small. I could have gone to my own sent mail file and printed out the proof that I had sent it, but even that seemed trivial.

A couple of days later, Rob called. "I found the original email," he said, "Sorry about that." I was glad to hear that it had turned up. And actually, we had a good discussion about his tendency to be somewhat rigid when he has an opinion and about how costly that might be for him in business and in relationships.

But the larger point is that sometimes it's a growth move to simply allow the other person to be wrong. The healthy people will eventually own up to any mistakes and come back to you to straighten things out. And regarding those who aren't so healthy, you can ask yourself, *Is it worth the effort and time to convince them that I'm right?* Even God doesn't go to infinite trouble to do that. Jesus was willingly "the stone the builders rejected" (Matthew 21:42); that is, he allowed the human race to disagree with what he claimed about himself. Let it go.

Relapse!

What if you find yourself losing yourself? I know that this is a little play on words, but there is a point here. We all relapse in the personal-growth arena. And with boundaries, it is common for a person to find herself "going along to get along" and losing her identity for the sake of peace in a relationship. For example, what if you begin to compromise your defining boundaries by shutting down emotionally, becoming compliant, sabotaging your freedom and choices, and losing your self-definition? Don't panic! Consider it part of learning and growing.

In my experience of helping people learn about boundaries, an occasional relapse is normal. Just as your physical workout progresses and regresses and your relationships improve and have glitches, so go your boundaries. Boundary development never goes in a straight line. Don't be discouraged. Just figure out what is going on. When you find that you are not defining yourself as you think you could be, most of the time it is caused by one of four issues: you have disconnected from support, you encounter resistance from someone you care about, you encounter resistance from your own self-talk, or you are taking risks in unfamiliar territory.

You Have Disconnected from Support

You may have run out of gas and spent too much time in isolation, in relationships that drain you, or in relationships that just don't offer a lot. Remember, your boundaries may be a little new and raw. They need TLC and people who affirm them in you. A person I was coaching told me, "I forgot to bond." I laughed because it sounded a little like, "I forgot to breathe." In time, learning to seek out support from those who are on your side will become a natural habit and not something you have to remember or make yourself do. But it often begins that way.

You Encounter Resistance from Someone You Care About

Not everyone is going to welcome your self-definition with open arms. You may be less controllable or more confrontive or more separate in your opinions. And someone who is important to you may resist the new "defined you." In some cases, he or she may even attack or judge you. There is no getting around the reality that this hurts. When someone matters to you, they have access to your more vulnerable parts. If they don't, they don't matter as much. And if they say things like, *You used to be so nice; you are selfish; you are trying to control me; you don't accept me; you are judging me,* that can make you think twice before trusting your own definition.

You may become hesitant about clarifying your values, thoughts, and emotions with others. Certainly, if someone questions your defining boundaries, you should always check out what is true and "first take the plank out of your own eye" (Matthew 7:5). We need to always be open to being wrong in a situation. Maybe you were the problem in the project at work. Maybe you came on too strong with your spouse at the party. Sometimes we can go overboard when we define ourselves and inadvertently try to control or even judge another person. We have nothing to fear from reality.

At the same time, if you have diligently looked at the plank in your eye, if you have checked out your perceptions—with God, the Bible, and wise people—and you have done your homework, then just stand firm when you get resistance from people about your opinion or boundary. This is the adult position. Let them be bugged with you. Love them. But don't give up what is right and true, either.

You Encounter Internal Resistance from Your Own Self-Talk

There is a part of you that has actively participated in not defining yourself. It presents itself as the voices in your head that constantly replay the dysfunctional tapes from your past. These are actually issues from old relationships that you've internalized; they slow your progress down, make you unsure, and add to your fear of being a defined person. You might find yourself thinking things like this: *I'm being mean; it's selfish to express my own opinions; I must be trying to control her; I must not be accepting her.*

Our inner life is highly impacted by our external connections with others, so these old tapes are echoes of past relational problems. Part of the purpose of your negative self-talk is *to keep you undefined and literally living in the past.* Believe it or not, the tapes that play in your head are actually trying to protect you. Your self-protective instincts know that if you stretch yourself, challenge others, and state who you are, you could be hurt again. Your mind reacts to past threats and reissues the self-talk so that you will not imperil yourself and suffer more damage. Obviously, this is a short-term gain that does you no good in the long run. When you hear the negative self-talk, recognize it for what it is; that will diminish its power. It is just the "old you" trying to protect you from the "new you."

You Are Taking Risks in Unfamiliar Territory

When you take your first steps to move beyond boundaries, you are stepping out on a limb. It's scary, and you aren't sure if it's safe to do so. It's a little like what happens to you when you challenge yourself in any new arena; you charge ahead only to find yourself afraid when you suddenly realize you aren't sure you know what you're doing.

I have an author friend who is a very good speaker, but speaking is not something for which she has always felt equipped or confident. She told me she spoke to a large group one day and had an almost out-of-body experience. She said, "I saw myself speaking to the group and thought, 'I am not qualified to be here.'" Fortunately, she mentally regrouped, and no one was the wiser.

You may have the same experience in trying to move beyond your boundaries. For example, you might think something like this: *telling the truth and setting a limit is not going to go well. I am going to catch a lot of trouble for this.* While that may be true, it's just as likely that you are taking healthy risks and experiencing some fear of the unknown as a result.

So expect relapse and pay attention to it. But don't get anxious. Realize that it is difficult to actually lose your defining boundaries. They become an essential part of you. Defining boundaries are the foundation that undergirds your protective boundaries. The more clear and honest you are with others about who you really are, the more ready you will be to move beyond boundaries and into the intimate connections you seek.

11

You Let Your Values Transform Your Desires

One of the greatest pleasures I get from working with people is when they tell me that they are moving up the food chain, relationally speaking. They are using better judgment in deciding whom to trust and why. Beyond that, it's a great joy when they tell me, "I'm not drawn to the type of person I used to be drawn to." Then I know that something transformational has happened. When you are actually attracted up the food chain and not just forcing yourself to do it, you are on the way to health and a great life.

I have a friend who recently attended his twentieth high school reunion. I asked him how it went. He said, "I talked to my high school sweetheart again after all these years. Man, what was I thinking back in the day?" He had gone for looks and personality, but part of her package was a deep self-absorption that he had not recognized as a teenager. At the time, he was only aware of how much he loved her and how hard it was when she refused to talk to him about anything he had going on.

He grew up and married a woman who was the whole package, including great character and an ability to get out of herself and into his world. He didn't really realize how much he had changed until he entered the reunion time warp, talked to his old girlfriend, and realized that she had not changed. She was still attractive and charming—and it was still all about her. He had a connect-the-dots experience, however. He was literally amazed that the attraction was no longer there. He saw her as someone he cared about, with a shared history and experiences, and actually someone he felt a bit sorry for, for her self-centeredness had led to some difficult losses for her. When he talked to his wife about the reunion, he felt inside how much he desired her and was attracted to her. As he said, "I realized that I won the relationship lottery."

You Need to Be Attracted to Health and Character

You can change whom you are attracted to. You can actually find yourself deeply drawn to better and healthier people. It happens all the time when the right elements are in place. And this is an important part of becoming ready to move beyond boundaries. The reason it is important is that in your next great relationship, *you need to be attracted to health and character.* This is true for any kind of relationship—romance, friendship, family, or business—and for new as well as existing connections.

Think about your protective boundaries for a moment. Why do they exist? Certainly, to keep you safe in a toxic situation. But beyond that, often part of the reason you have had to set limits, distance yourself, establish consequences, and be firm with someone in the first place is because of a character defect in that individual. So it doesn't do well for you to continue being attracted to poor character and then go to all the work of setting protective limits again. I have worked with too many people who miss this part and end up with the same type of person, just with a different last name. You don't want to repeat that pattern—and you don't have to when you change whom you are attracted to by becoming a person of health and character.

Sometimes I hear people talk about their unhealthy relationships as if their bad patterns are a genetic inevitability: "I'll always be vulnerable to charming and manipulative people, so I need to always be on guard." *No! Not true!*

You are not doomed to some sort of permanent addiction to bad relationships that you need to cope with the rest of your life. You really can be attracted, at a deep level, to health and maturity. You were designed that way. God has a win-win in mind: people do enjoy a healthy meal that also tastes good. Here is how you can do better than coping: let your values transform your desires. That is, identify what is really important to you at the deepest level and begin living out those values. You will see the difference. God designed the process, so that you may "be transformed by the renewing of your mind" (Romans 12:2).

You may have heard how bank tellers are trained to spot counterfeit bills. They don't learn a lot about ink types, printing, or paper categories. Instead, for weeks they are given nothing but real bills to handle, thousands of them in all denominations. They touch and look at the bills over and over again. They immerse themselves in the real thing. Then when a counterfeit passes through their hands, they just know, in a sixth-sense kind of way, that *this is different*. It is not what they're used to. From that point on, they do further checking and confirm the fraud.

In a similar way, the more you immerse yourself in good health and character—become who you really are, live out what you believe in, and relate to others on that level—the more you will recognize and experience the *real thing*. The real thing works. Health breeds a better life. And your relational system begins looking for that.

But you can't tell your feelings and tastes to change. You must go deeper, into the soil of who you are. You must first address your values.

Values That Transform Desires

As you decide on what is most important to you, it must be more than a list in a frame on the wall. Your values must be something you think about all through your life, that you talk about with people, and that dictate your behaviors and attitudes. As your values become healthier and more righteous, you will find yourself drawn to healthier and more righteous people, who have similar values.

Here are three core values that will help you be, and find, the right person.

Live Out the Value of Following God

God is the center of the universe and of your life. As Rick Warren says, "It's not about you."[6] It's about God. Seek his ways and his guidance. The healthiest life is also the holiest life, because holiness is living a life set apart (that is, clearly defined) for God's use. There are three core values that God has told us to follow, which, if you make them part of your life, will change your desires and attractions at a deep level. They will help you be drawn to the right people, because holiness and health are drawn to holiness and health.

I was speaking recently at a singles retreat, and a woman named Marcie said, "I'm a Christian, and I'm dating a man who doesn't share my faith. Otherwise, he connects very well with me, he is honest, and he has great character. Should I break up with him?"

"It depends," I said. "Is this a beginning relationship for you, one in which you're just getting out into the dating world?"

"No," she said, "it's more than that."

"How would you describe it?"

"I'm in love with him."

"So you are so into him that you might want to marry him?"

"Yes."

"Okay, Marcie, let's play the tape forward. He has some terrific qualities that you love and appreciate, so you get married. Although there are great parts of the connection, you go to church alone. You pray and read your Bible alone—no couples' devotions. You are in a small group by yourself while he stays home. And the deepest, most core parts of you have to go to other relationships because, even though you love each other, the spiritual connection is not there. That doesn't make him a bad guy. It just means you have a problem."

She was a quick study and very values-driven. It took her about three seconds, and she said, "I get it. I've got to break up with him. My faith is what I'm about."

Marcie was tearing up, and I felt sad for her, but she got it. Not that she thought herself better or him inferior. And not that she wasn't going to hurt over this. But she was living out her values. She didn't say, "I'm not attracted to him anymore," because it sounded as if he had some healthy, attractive qualities. But she knew that she would only be happiest and most complete when her deepest values were lived out in a relationship.

I have seen many people like her who made the hard choice she knew she needed to make and later found themselves connected to someone they could share their lives with—spiritually, emotionally, and physically. However, if it means staying single, that is okay as well. When Peter asked Jesus, "Lord, to whom shall we go? You have the words of eternal life" (John 6:68), he was affirming the reality that the only life that makes sense is the life fully committed to, and fully engaged with, God. Once you know God and his words of eternal life, you are imprinted and see that there really is no viable alternative.

Living out this value helps transform your desires. To want God and his paths in every part of your life also means you want the important people in your life to connect with you on that level. It's a little like what happens in the physical world when you get serious about working out and eating right. You do it long enough, and the chips just aren't quite as much of a draw as something healthier. Play the tape of the future, as Marcie did. As she put all the realities together, she became sad. She was already loosening her hold on the relationship, grieving, and allowing her desires to change.

Live Out the Value of Vulnerable Relationships

If relationship is one of God's primary delivery systems for providing what we need, it makes sense that relationship should be a high value for you. There are few experiences more positive and rewarding than knowing someone and being known at a deep level. Once you have this experience, it's easy to get used to it and ultimately to require it for yourself. When you have experienced that sort of empathic grace, you realize it is an essential for you.

That is what happened to my friend who attended his high school reunion. When he first met the woman who is now his wife, he didn't know why he had such a great time with her. Then, as he thought about it, he realized it was because she connected with him. As they moved on in the relationship, she really listened to what he said and focused on him. Not only that, but she moved toward his losses and insecurities as much as she did his accomplishments and dreams. She wanted to know his weaknesses as well as his strengths.

In turn, she was vulnerable with him about her own weaknesses. She didn't need to pretend to have it all together. And he was drawn to those parts of her. Neither of them is perfect; they have their dark sides. But they have removed their fig leaves with each other as much as they can. And those years of intimacy made the contrast to the high school relationship stark. He is drawn to depth, to safety, to acceptance, to active listening. His relational tastes have changed.

You don't have to marry someone to experience this kind of transformation. But you do have to find some context in which this is happening, be it with friends or family. Once you have been deeply connected and accepted, it's hard to settle for less. It is too fulfilling to walk away from.

Live Out the Value of Honesty

People who have lived in a difficult relationship often learn how to distort reality as a coping mechanism. They have encountered in the other person a character flaw or a habit pattern that is deeply embedded and shows no sign of changing. Yet they care about the person and don't want to leave the relationship. Without being aware of it, they compromise certain truths to avoid feeling divided or inconsistent or hypocritical. It is the same thing you do when you try on a pair of pants that are now too tight and say, "The cleaners must have shrunk my pants." This form of rationalizing reality makes things more tolerable, at least in the short term.

For example, you may have put up with someone who is a chronic blamer for a long time. Whatever the problem, this person made it your fault, even in the face of black-and-white evidence to the contrary. I once worked with Rebecca, a corporate executive, whose sales manager, Aaron, was talented in people skills but nevertheless suffered from the blame disease. Rebecca appreciated Aaron's competencies, but the blaming behavior drove her crazy. If there was a personnel problem, a financial glitch, or a scheduling conflict, Aaron always made it someone else's fault—be it Rebecca, the bad traffic, his ex-wife, or the economy.

We were talking about business one day, and I asked Rebecca how it was going with Aaron. "Actually, things are better," she said. "I don't think he is as bad as he used to be." Encouraged, I said, "That's great, what happened?" Unfortunately, what she ended up telling me was that she tried not to think about the blaming and instead made herself the bad guy most of the time. That was how she bent and morphed reality in order to live with it.

"Oh, I knew he wouldn't look at the report the right way, so I just took over; it's fine, he's a nice guy." She smiled indulgently, the way some codependent moms smile when their six-year-old misbehaves in the grocery store, as if to say, *Oh, that little stinker, but isn't he darling?*

I was a little alarmed and said so. "This isn't okay," I said, "You need some direct talks here, valuable employee or not. He might change. But even if he doesn't, at least you and he will know the reality and have to deal with it."

Rebecca got over her fear and lived out her honesty, for she truly did value honesty. She was just afraid. She had direct conversations with Aaron about his blaming behaviors. Things got better for a while, but he eventually got tired of the scrutiny and left. But here is the happy ending. There were plenty of sales managers waiting for interviews who were at least as talented as Aaron. And Rebecca, after some bumps transitioning between employees, was much better off with her new hire. She had a competent person who also took responsibility for mistakes.

And there was yet another and perhaps even greater benefit for Rebecca. She has developed an internal "no tolerance" policy with blamers. When she hears a pattern of excuses, she quickly confronts it and deals with it. She is not a mean person at all; in fact, she is quite kind. But she really doesn't put up with blame anymore. Her tastes have changed. No more indulgent smiles. Friendliness, yes, and high expectations, yes. But the draw toward excusing and excuser has disappeared.

Dare to be honest. Tell the truth. It is a value for you, but one that needs to be exercised in your life. Using it prevents you from trying to adjust reality in order to fit a bad situation. Once the truth is out, either you will help the other person change or you will face the matter squarely and adapt in a healthier way. And you will find that you are more attracted to people of the truth, the way you have become a person of the truth.

When you become more honest about what is true and real, you are actually recalibrating "normal" in your mind. You probably have accepted some patterns you didn't know were destructive because they were all you knew. A fish doesn't know it's wet because wet is the only thing it knows. I recently talked with a couple about their early relationship. He told me he had a "Mommy Dearest" mother who was loving one day and a screaming rageaholic the next. His dad never confronted the behavior, so the man actually thought that being yelled at for no reason was part of a normal mother-son relationship. He didn't begin to see it differently until his early married years when his wife witnessed one of her mother-in-law's rage attacks and was shocked. His wife said, "This is crazy and wrong. I won't have this around our marriage and our kids."

He was confused about this. But his wife's normal reaction to abnormality was enough to get him thinking about how normal love, kindness, patience, and self-control were—as well as the possibility that his mom was crazy. That led to his own personal and relational growth as a man, husband, and father. And like Rebecca, he became much clearer about what he liked and disliked in a relationship.

Be the kind of person you want to be attracted to. You will find that you are less and less drawn to people with difficult character issues and more desirous to find people who are full of grace, safety, acceptance, and a hunger to grow.

12

You Know Which Risks Are Worth Taking and Which Are Not

Great relationships are fulfilling.

Great relationships involve risk.

You can't have the first without the second.

Great relationships require that you be open to taking risks —risks of being misunderstood, of alienation, of someone being hurt by you as well. It doesn't mean relationships aren't worth the risks, for the good ones are. It is simply the price of the course. No pain, no gain.

The challenge is that people who have been burnt in a relationship often have trouble with risk. They get out of balance. Sometimes they insist on no risk and try to control the course of the relationship. This can actually be boring and unfulfilling. And sometimes they allow behavior that is unacceptable in the name of taking risks. In other words, they don't quite know the difference between risks that are worth taking and risks that are not worth taking. In order to move beyond boundaries and prepare yourself for openness and vulnerability, you have to clarify which risks are—and are not—worth taking.

Risk, Love, and Freedom

A risk is simply the possibility of danger. Taking a risk means you make a choice knowing that you cannot control an outcome. It could be in any area of life: finances, physical activities, or relationships. When you are jogging on a road, you risk being hit by a car. When you move off the road onto the grass, you risk stepping into a hole and twisting your ankle. So you measure the risk in light of the potential gain. Every day we make these calculated judgments, in ways both small and large. The same is true in relationships. When a man walks up to a woman at a party and introduces himself, he takes a risk that she will not be interested. When the woman responds, she risks that he may, in turn, then back off.

Yet, risk is the only path we have to experience truly satisfying relationships. The way it is supposed to work is that over a gradual process, both people peel back the onion layers of who they are, eventually getting to the deeper levels. That is where great friendships, dating relationships, and marriages are headed. But there is a catch, which is what risk is all about: *healthy connections always give the other person a choice.* This is the possibility of danger. If you are interested in someone, if you are invested in someone, if you love someone, you must allow that person freedom. They can choose to not reciprocate your love, to be uncaring, and to end the relationship. And you must guard their freedom to do this. It is the only way you, or anyone else, will truly experience love.

Love cannot exist without freedom. No one can give himself to another at an authentic level if he doesn't have a choice. It is meaningless to have another person be with you out of fear, obligation, or pity. What would that experience be like for you? You would feel empty and isolated. You would not feel connected. You would most likely pull away from the relationship. Love can't be commanded or coerced; it can only be given.

A friend of mine, Richard Gonzalez, leads a large, small-group-based ministry at a church in the Los Angeles area. He helps husbands who have mistreated their wives and whose wives, as a consequence, have left them. The men come to him broken and with no idea how to repair things. He says, "The first thing I tell them is to stop texting and calling their wives. Most of the time, they are overwhelming their wives with constant appeals to return — begging, pleading, and trying to make them feel guilty. I tell them, you are trying to control your wife, which is what got the relationship in trouble in the first place. Stop this and start working on yourself, for yourself — not to get her back. Then let her find out that you are a new man."

Richard is highly successful in this approach. He gets to the heart of the matter, which is that no one can truly open up for any reason other than their free choice to do so.

Love cannot be coerced when you have been the one at fault. Nor can it be coerced when you are the innocent party. A man I know has a drug-addicted adult son. The young man is full of resentment toward his dad because, after years of enabling the addiction, the dad set a limit and stopped his codependency. He had been paying for the young man's living expenses, with no requirement that his son seek help. When the father told his son that he would no longer fund living expenses without rehab, the young man became angry and accused his dad of being uncaring. The son left the relationship and would not speak to his dad. Actually, the limits were the most caring thing the father had done in a long time, but the son couldn't see it that way.

The dad was hurt and wounded by his son's disconnection. He was tempted to cave in and get back in his son's good graces by renewing the financial support. He came close to doing so because of how much he missed his son. But he steeled himself and simply told the young man, "I will not pay for anything except rehab. If you choose to do that and it is successful, I'm willing to talk further about helping you." He told his son that ultimately, even if he became drug free, he should, at some point, be paying his own way, so he was making no promises.

The dad had to tolerate his son's hatred for several years, and it was hard on him. Finally, the son fell in love with a young woman, and she insisted he get help. She mattered more to him than his dad did, and he listened to her. He entered a program. As often happens, during the program, he realized how unfair he had been to his dad, and they began a process of reconciliation. It has been a slow process, but it has been worth it to the father. The dad could have "paid for" his son's positive response to him, but he knew it would not have been love. It would have been no more than a transaction, empty and without meaning or life.

This is why, over and over again, God asks us to seek him from our hearts, the deepest parts of us: "But if from there you seek the LORD your God, you will find him if you seek for him with all your heart and with all your soul" (Deuteronomy 4:29). God has no interest in fear-based obedience; he knows it has no meaning. God wants to be loved, and he made you in his image so that you also want to be loved. But love never develops without freedom, and so there is always risk.

Distinguish between Acceptable and Unacceptable Risks

If you were run over, so to speak, by the freedom of someone you cared about, all of this talk about risk might be hard for you. You may be risk-averse, and no one could blame you. It can be confusing at first, especially on the tail end of a bad relationship. I saw this in a man I worked with who came from a harsh and controlling family. Nick had few choices as a boy and had adopted a compliant personality style to survive his childhood. He just toed the line to make it from day to day and never expressed his real thoughts and feelings. His compliance pattern worked for him, and he learned to channel his energies into being a business success. He worked great in authoritarian structures, where the boss was strict and rigid. But he felt dead inside, and he knew it was a problem.

In our work together, Nick became aware of how much legitimate personal power and control he had never had. As often happens, when he got in touch with those feelings, he went through a season of becoming controlling himself, sort of turning the tables. Actually, it was a way for him to separate himself enough from the controlling dad in his mind, to become more comfortable with his own power. But during this season, he was hard to live with. When his wife disagreed with him about a financial decision he made, for example, this normally easygoing guy said, "If you loved me, you would support and trust me." In other words, he interpreted her freedom as a lack of love and as something that was not good for him.

But here is the reality: *the problem is never the freedom. The problem is always the character of two people: yours and the person you love.* Don't make freedom the bad guy;

instead, you must celebrate and protect it, because without it there is no love. But you get hurt either because the person was unloving, there was a miscommunication, or you allowed something you shouldn't have, or because you wanted something that wasn't possible. So that leads us to risk again. If risk is inevitable and even a good thing, you need to understand the difference between risks that are acceptable and those that are not.

Hurt and Harm

Can you tell the difference between when you are hurt and when you are harmed in a relationship? There is a large gap between discomfort and actual damage to your emotional well-being. Discomfort may be acceptable but damage never is. The experience of pain may be the same, so it's sometimes hard to tell from that perspective. In fact, there may be less pain in a bad, harmful risk than there is in an acceptable risk. You have to look at different factors.

For example, suppose you lend a friend $20 because he is having a cash problem. This is a risk, but unless you are in a precarious financial situation yourself, it is not a harmful risk. Then suppose your friend just ignores his debt to you out of his own self-absorption or general flakiness. It may annoy or hurt you, but you have not been harmed. However, if he fails to pay you back after you give him your life savings because he doesn't want to get a job—then you have experienced harm.

The reason this is important is that one of the unfortunate consequences of a bad relationship is that an individual can develop an abnormally high pain threshold. She may not know when she is being hurt or when she is being harmed. In some cases, she may not even be aware that anything negative is happening at all. She tolerates behaviors, attitudes, and words she should not put up with. She literally does not feel what is happening to her, almost as if she were relationally anesthetized.

I observed a couple at a party who showed this dynamic. In front of other people, he made a joke and called her a dog. To my astonishment and sadness, she then said, "Woof-woof." In the guise of being a good sport, she allowed what she should not have allowed. At some level she may have been aware that it was damaging because she then made a comment about how she is an open person and has thick skin. I suppose that is possible. But for my money, she was humiliated by the man who supposedly loved her.

Living in a state of relational anesthesia occurs slowly over time. You try to be the bigger person, the grown-up. You try not to overreact emotionally. You don't want to be a whiner or be seen as high maintenance or sensitive. Or you simply get used to it and try to ignore it, so that you can function in the relationship without a lot of emotional conflict. In the end, this is not good for you. You need to feel good when you are loved and bad when you are mistreated. Then you are in touch with yourself and with reality, and you can make better decisions about your relationship.

If relational anesthesia is an issue for you, you aren't yet ready for a great deal of vulnerability. You may take some risks that could cause problems and never see them coming. Pay attention to your emotions, especially the negative ones. They exist to protect you and serve as a signal to you of what's going on.[7] It may be that you are being treated well or poorly. But you are responsible to tell the difference.

Discerning the Difference

How do you discern the difference between a hurtful result and a harmful result when you take a risk? Here's the distinction: while hurt is the experience of something painful, it may not be damaging. But harm is different. *Harm creates significant problems in the three primary areas of life.* Let's see how this plays out.

Withdrawal from other relationships. If your experience in the relationship affects how you relate to other people in a significantly negative way, this is a sign of harm. For example, suppose you fall in love. You were vulnerable with that person and took risks in the attachment. You let yourself depend on her and let her know you at a deeper level. Then you experienced a conflict, and it became unsafe to continue being emotionally open with her. If you are sad and discouraged about that, you have experienced hurt. Though not enjoyable, that is normal in a relationship. However, if you are now unable to reach out and let others in, isolate yourself from people, and withdraw from support, that is harm. The difficult relationship caused damage that impacts your other relationships, and you need time and attention to heal.

Personal decline. Your personal life encompasses everything that happens inside your skin: your behaviors, how you feel about yourself, your emotional well-being, and your habits. Taking the same example of falling in love, if the relational conflict results in any kind of sustained personal decline—for example, depression, significant weight change, or incapacitating self-doubt—that is harm.

Diminished performance. Performance has to do with the *doing* aspects of life, the tasks and activities. Your job, career, financial life, home organization, and time management are parts of the performance piece. Harm happens when you can no longer function at the same levels you did or find that you can start projects and tasks but can't finish them. Often, a person will experience problems in energy, focus, creativity, or enjoyment of work.

Luke, a small-business owner whom I coached, entered a tumultuous period with his wife. She was extremely possessive and would fly off the handle when he wanted to spend time with his friends. The energy drain that came from the marriage was so large that he found himself making strategic and financial mistakes at the office. He literally could not perform at the level he had for many years. The relationship was causing harm. If you are finding that work is not what it used to be, it may not be the job. It may be a relational drain you are experiencing.

Are you starting to see the difference between hurt and harm more clearly? Does it give you a better idea of the kinds of risks that routinely come with connection and the kinds of risks that should never be taken? Here are some additional examples to help make the difference crystal clear:

- It is acceptable to have an argument, but not to be yelled at and treated with contempt.

- It is acceptable to pick the wrong person, but not to let that person take over your life, thoughts, and values.

- It is acceptable to open up to a person and feel bad if they become critical of you, but not to allow it to happen repeatedly.

- It is acceptable to give up controlling the outcome of the relationship and where it will end up, but not to let the other person's choices be the only choices.

When problems happen in a relationship, keep pushing through hurt, as long as you are committed to the relationship. But pay attention to when things cross the line into harm.

Assess the Return on Your Relational Investment

Aside from looking at hurt and harm, ask yourself, *Is the relationship worth the time and energy I put into it?* Some relationships are and some are not. You only have so much time and energy. You need to steward your time well just as you need to steward your finances well. When you buy stocks or invest in a business, you expect a return on your investment. The same is true in relationships; something good should happen—increased love, connection, intimacy, building a life together.

It may be an acceptable risk of your time and energy to hang in there with a friendship that is struggling, because you believe in the person or because you see a light at the end of the tunnel. Or it may not. I see this problem often among people who are navigating the singles world. A woman will be dating a man, and it seems to be a perfectly normal relationship. Then I find out that he is commitment-phobic and that they have been dating for six years. There is nothing crazy, mean, or abusive going on; no harm that is apparent. But if the woman is hoping for marriage and a family, this situation is likely not an acceptable risk of her time and energy.

The clearer you are about what you want in a relationship, what you are willing to invest, and how much may be too much, the better off you'll be. The line that you draw is the line between acceptable and unacceptable risk.

Move Past Generalization

When risks go the wrong way, another problem occurs. Let me explain. There is a phrase that, after reading this book, I hope you will never say again. It is this: "You just can't trust X." The X can be men, divorced men, women, single women, charming personality types, the human race, or an infinite number of groups. I assure you that you will have a happier life and will move beyond self-protection into relationship if you forever delete this phrase from your vocabulary.

"You just can't trust *them*," comes from a psychological concept called *generalization*. Generalization is the act of deriving principles from isolated experiences. The individual takes a few experiences of someone from one group and assumes that every person in that group is the same way:

- Men are unable to make an emotional attachment.
- Women are manipulative.
- Single men are self-absorbed.
- Divorced women are desperate.
- Sooner or later, people will let you down.

The reality, however, is that while there will always be some toxic people around, no group is 100 percent populated with untrustworthy individuals. Think about yourself, for example. You would not want to be stereotyped into some untrue tendency because you are in a certain demographic group. You would not want someone to judge you that way and presume you are guilty before finding out if you are innocent.

Why do we generalize? There are two main reasons — for self-protection and to simplify complexity. People often generalize as a form of self-protection when boundaries are violated. They reason that if you swear off all members of a group representative of the person who hurt you, you are less likely to be hurt again. It's rarely an intentional choice. It is a simple association that occurs in the more primitive parts of our brains. We see someone similar to the negative person, and our self-protective instincts tell us to move away.

We also generalize because it simplifies life decisions. Kids learn that a person who is smiling is more likely to be kind than someone who is shouting. You can write off a gender, a socioeconomic group, a religion, or a personality style without having to take a risk. Rather than entering into the due diligence of dealing with the complexities of who people are, the broad swipe becomes a black-and-white way of keeping matters easy to classify. And people who have trust issues typically prefer to find some way to disqualify a new relationship rather than to risk damage by making a poor judgment call. Better safe than sorry.

Actually, when I am working with a true rescuer — someone who trusts too quickly and ends up enabling others' self-destructive behaviors — I go easy on him at first and don't say much about his generalizations. Sometimes generalizations may be a sign of progress! It's preferable to letting someone do anything she wants to you at any time and never calling her destructiveness what it is. So when the rescuer moves beyond, "He blew up at me because he is under stress at work," to "Men just use women to vent their frustrations," I will allow the person a little time to hang on to her angry, unrealistic, and unfair generalization before clarifying it. But at some point it needs to be addressed and worked out.

If you find that you have a pattern of generalizing, you are most likely reacting to hurt, and you must deal with it and get healing for it. Even if your generalizations come from an injured place, you are still judging someone. This is not fair to anyone—either yourself or the other person. The answer to this is to *use judgment instead of judging.* That is, evaluate another person based on their own words and actions over time rather than stereotyping them based on a previous destructive relationship. This will help you move beyond your protective boundaries, and you will find more opportunities for authentic connection.

Consider generalization as a temporary boundary. It keeps you from harm and risk. It guards your heart. But it is ultimately not going to serve you well. So the best answer is to keep developing your own boundaries, your ability to say yes and no in love, and to be truthful. Then you will be confident in your abilities to take care of yourself in relationships, and you will enjoy getting to know those people you might otherwise have passed over.

A woman I worked with, who had been severely mistreated by an angry, aggressive husband, went into a season after her divorce in which, for a while, she saw all men as untrustworthy. They were either "control freaks" and "dominating" or "immature little boys" and "whiners." She swore off dating for a while, which I supported, because it gave her focus and energy to do a thorough recovery of her life, emotions, and thoughts. In time, however, she began to be interested in men again. This time, her generalizations were more specific. She liked some men, but anyone who was energetic, confrontive, or a take-charge person was shoved into the "controlling and abusive" category. She allowed that there were men who could be loving, sensitive, and safe, but they couldn't have any aggressive qualities.

So she dated a few passive men, thinking that was the

answer. But as you might guess from reading this description of her own up-front nature, she quickly became disinterested. Not enough energy and definition. Finally, however, she became secure enough that her antennae found a man who was full of love and full of truth. They had some spats, but she did not stereotype him. She understood that if she wanted to be honest and clear, she had to accept and support that behavior in a man as well. She continued opening herself to the relationship and getting past her fear. They did not marry, but it wasn't because she generalized the man she was dating. They simply had different paths in life.

If you have been the trusting, naïve sort, you may simply have to generalize for a while, just to start thinking in categories. Children learn that there are good guys and bad guys on TV. The good-looking, clean-cut one is good, and the ugly one is bad. They are establishing buckets, or categories, to make sense of the world.

If you don't have buckets, you may need to have some broad way to make sense of things, as your discernment gets better. But realize that generalizations are temporary. No one should be judged guilty until proven innocent, especially anyone with whom you might want to have a relationship, or anyone you might be attracted to but need an excuse to get away from. Get past the generalizations and into the individual.

Risk is unavoidable, but you can begin to distinguish between risks that hurt and risks that harm. And even if your experience has been harmful, do what you need to do to get past generalizations. There are a lot of good people in the world to connect with as you move beyond boundaries.

PART 3

KNOWING WHEN THE OTHER PERSON IS READY

When you let your needs for attachment trump your values, you are headed for problems. However, when your values trump your needs for attachment, you are headed in the right direction. Moving beyond boundaries requires understanding what to value and look for in the other person before you become vulnerable and attached. There is a due-diligence process that will help you know how to determine if the other person is ready for a relationship. At the beginning, you won't know where this connection will lead. You could end up with a great friendship, a business partnership, or even a marriage. Who knows? But you can know a great deal about whether the person is ready for the two of you to pursue and explore it.

You may be interested in a new person, or you may be looking at an existing relationship on which you previously set limits and now must determine if the person is "new" and changed in the right ways. Some of the chapters in part 3 have to do with the other person's process of growth, healing, and maturity. Others address how toxic or safe the person is. But every chapter will equip you to more smoothly navigate the relational waters beyond boundaries.

13

Does This Person Care about His or Her Impact on You?

A friend of mine wanted to get into the arena of public speaking. She had a great deal of professional expertise and accomplishment and was at the point in her career in which she wanted to deliver it to audiences. She asked me for help. I contacted another friend who was networked with an organization that put on speaking events because I thought his contacts would be a good fit for her. He was helpful and offered to give her contact information for the decision makers.

Several months later, the three of us happened to be at the same professional conference. I asked the two of them how the speaking possibility was going. She said nothing was happening and that no one had responded to her emails and phone calls. I felt bad that her efforts seemed wasted. My networking friend said, "It wasn't me. I contacted the people myself, so whatever broke down, it wasn't me." My speaker friend looked a little discouraged but said nothing. I felt bad for her again because of what he said. His response showed that he was not really concerned about her disappointment.

The energy went to his fear of being the bad guy or being perceived as the person at fault.

He and I talked later, and since he is basically a good person, he understood how his comment affected my friend. He hadn't even been aware of how he had come across and felt bad about it. He apologized to her for the gaffe. I have done the same thing myself, so I understood. But here is the part that matters to you as you move beyond boundaries: *the people you are ready to risk with must be concerned about their impact on you.* They must care about how they affect you, for better or for worse.

The Reality of Relational Impact

We matter to each other. If someone is significant to you, how she behaves, speaks, values, thinks, and feels toward you will impact you. That is how we are designed by God. We get inside each other and make a difference. God tells us in many ways to be aware of how we respond to each other. Look at the verses that follow and how they first teach us how to treat each other. Then they tell us the impact we have based on how we treat each other.

- "I appeal to you, brothers and sisters, in the name of our Lord Jesus Christ, that all of you agree with one another in what you say and that there be no divisions among you, but that you be perfectly united in mind and thought" (1 Corinthians 1:10). In other words, we have the power to divide our relationships, or to unite them with each other.

- "But encourage one another daily, as long as it is called 'Today,' so *that none of you may be hardened* by sin's deceitfulness" (Hebrews 3:13, emphasis added). We impact one another to the extent to which we mutually encourage each other. Without that, we run the risk of becoming hardened.

- "Therefore confess your sins to each other and pray for each other so *that you may be healed*" (James 5:16, emphasis added). A powerful verse, illustrating that we play a role in actually healing each other.

- "Above all, love each other deeply, because *love covers over a multitude of sins*" (1 Peter 4:8, emphasis added). Our love for each other helps deal with the sins we commit.

We can initiate division or end it; indulge sin or resist it; harden each other or soften each other; heal or not heal; cover sins or leave them as they are. We matter to each other.

Psychological theory and research supports this principle as well. When I conduct diagnostic interviews with new clients, most of my time is spent on getting information about their significant relationships, present and past. I know that if I find patterns of how important people related to them, I will understand a great deal about why they suffer the way they do.

Your life certainly attests to this. If you were to identify the top five impacts on your life—the things that have strongly formed the person you are today—most of them would likely involve people: your parents and how they related to you; a teacher or coach who inspired you; your romantic relationships, in dating or marriage; a long-term business relationship or a mentor. We are deeply shaped and impacted by the significant people in our lives.

Why You Need People to Care about Their Impact on You

The extent to which other people are concerned about their impact on you is the extent to which you can trust them. You trust them because you know it's not just you looking after yourself; they are looking after you too. He wants to make sure he is treating you with care and respect. She expends energy thinking about how her words might wound you or lift you up. He cares how his anger might scare you; how his immaturity might let you down; how his ability to listen might give you hope and encouragement. When you trust a person, you let down your guard, relax, and become yourself. You are care-*less*. You don't worry about reading his mind. You don't have to anticipate her next move or worry about her criticizing you because you let her see you make a mistake. You are just yourself.

I don't mean that you should require a person to be a mind reader, so that he will never make a mistake with you. This is impossible. It does mean, however, that if he hurts you and you let him know, he will be *more concerned about your well-being than his own comfort*. He will want to know what he did, how it affected you, and how he needs to change. He will even feel protective toward you. For example, I was working with Steve and Lisa on learning this, so that they could connect on a deeper level. She had a tendency to criticize him in public. It wasn't mean or harsh. It was more like he was always the idiot in her stories: how he dented the car, got the flight info wrong, let their daughter wrap him around her finger, and so on. He brought it up in the session. Here is how the conversation went:

Steve: "Sometimes I dread going to a party with you because I know I'll be the butt of one of your stories."

Lisa: "I'm sorry, but it's not that bad, and I don't mean any harm."

John: "If I heard you tell me that, I would emotionally shut down right now."

Steve: "Yes. I just did."

Lisa: "Why? I was just explaining ..."

John: "You were explaining. And you may even be right. Maybe he is oversensitive, but at this point that's irrelevant."

Lisa: "But I didn't mean anything ..."

John: "I know. You weren't trying to bug him. But here is what I wanted you to say: 'I didn't know I had that effect. I don't want you to dread going places with me. Tell me more about what happens; I want to understand this.' "

Lisa (to Steve): "Is that true? Is that what you want?"

Steve: "Yes."

John: "When you say things like 'It's not that bad' and 'I don't mean any harm,' it sounds as if you care more about him understanding you are a good person than you care about how you affect him with your jokes."

Lisa: "I do want him to realize I have good motives."

John: "More than you care about how you make him feel?"

Lisa (pause): "No."

John: "Sure?"

Lisa: "Yes, I'm sure. But I just hate thinking that he will misunderstand me and think I'm a bad person."

John (to Steve): "Why don't you speak to her concern?"

Steve: "I may misunderstand you, and if I do, let me know. But it really makes it better for me when you care about how you affect me; and it makes it worse for me when you care more about image management. I love you, and I think you are a great person."

John (to Lisa): "What if the tables were turned? For example, I know that you don't like it when he gets really mad and is loud with you and the kids."

Lisa: "But that's a bad thing; he shouldn't do that anyway."

John: "I understand. But remember when I agreed with you about that, and he had to listen to how that scares you, and then he felt bad?"

Lisa: "He started crying."

John: "He started crying. He had no idea what his anger was doing to you, and he felt a lot of remorse for putting you and the kids through those nightmares."

Lisa: "I get it. I'm sorry, Honey. I want to get you like you got me."

Steve was right. He married a good person. But Lisa had to come to terms with a problem many of us have: we value how we are perceived more than the impact we have on others. She got the message, however. Lisa was a mild case. Had she fought me and insisted she was innocent and never gotten to wondering about her impact on Steve, I would have been more concerned. But she got to the right place.

Was Steve overreacting? Actually, as I got to know him, probably so. He tended to be oversensitive to slights, and I had him work on this issue, as it wasn't her fault, and he needed to improve in that area. The point is, however, that you need to be a person who cares about how you affect others and require that of those who matter to you.

To clarify all this, here are some additional examples of caring and uncaring responses people have in various situations:

Situation: A husband is overspending, and his wife mentions the problem to him.

Uncaring response: I have a right to the money as much as you do. I can choose, and you need to trust me.

Caring response: I didn't know how much the spending scared you. Let's look at the budget and figure something out.

Situation: An adult child is living with his parents, and it's time to get a job and move out.

Uncaring response: Get off my back, you guys are so unsupportive!

Caring response: I appreciate the break you're giving me. Let's come up with a launch plan that works.

Situation: A wife is chronically late, and the husband has brought it up.

Uncaring response: You're always micromanaging me.

Caring response: I guess it's hard when I tell you I'll be home at 6:00 for dinner, and it's always 6:45.

Situation: A direct report is not attuned to the culture of his organization, and the team is suffering because of it.

Uncaring response: I'm doing my best. You don't see the things I do for this company.

Caring response: Tell me what I'm doing, I want to fix this.

Situation: A husband has a critical mom, and his wife is getting the brunt of it.

Uncaring response: Just be nice to my mom and stop griping.

Caring response: I'm sorry for not standing up to my mom when she criticizes you.

Situation: A friend takes a long time to repay a loan.

Uncaring response: I don't think you realize all the things I do for you.

Caring response: I'm really sorry. I haven't been up on this with you. How soon do you need it?

Situation: A husband's drinking is concerning his wife.

Uncaring response: If you wouldn't disrespect me, I wouldn't have to drink; it's my way of coping with you.

Caring response: I am so sorry I scare you when I drink. I'll never drink like that again, and if I do, tell me, and I'll get help.

Don't give up hope if you are getting uncaring responses. It may not be a sign to find the exit door. The person you're interested in connecting with might just need a little coaching. Then they understand that it's important to you to know how they affect you. But don't take any more steps toward vulnerability until you talk about this. If it's a little defensiveness or cluelessness and the lights come on when you talk about it, and their behavior begins to change, then they pass that test and it's safe to proceed.

I hope you understand that you aren't being selfish or a whiner to want this. Desiring and, ultimately, requiring that someone be concerned about his or her impact on you is not a matter of self-absorption or "it's all about me." It is your responsibility and evidence of self-stewardship. You only have one heart, and that heart is the core of you. If you repeatedly subject it to bad treatment, constantly have to protect yourself, or realize you are the only one in the relationship who is concerned about you, you are not taking good care of that heart.

The Bible makes it clear how important this is: "Above all else, guard your heart, for everything you do flows from it" (Proverbs 4:23). In an intimate relationship, you need to guard your heart, and you want the other person to guard your heart as well. You wouldn't send your kids to a school where the teacher took no responsibility for them. Nor would you entrust your investments to a financial advisor who repeatedly mismanaged them. Make guarding your heart—and expecting others to do the same—a part of what you want and expect in a meaningful connection.

Is Behavior Change Enough?

Some people think it's unreasonable to expect more from the other person than a change of behavior. They don't want to be demanding or perfectionistic, so they settle for external modifications rather than internal changes in the other person. For example, it's enough that the excessive drinker, though not showing concern, cuts back on the booze without attending a twelve-step program. The emotionally disconnected person says nothing about it, but turns off the TV and talks more. The self-absorbed person doesn't acknowledge the dynamic, but tries to listen to your point of view. Should behavior changes such as these be enough?

I don't want to be a wet blanket, but no. When the person

changes behavior, but you see no evidence that the change is due to a heart-level understanding of how the person impacted you, most likely what you are seeing is compliance. You are not seeing transformation. Compliance is about getting caught and not wanting to get caught again. It does not develop trust.

When I leave half a sandwich too close to the edge of the kitchen table and walk to another room, it is about 95 percent certain that one of my dogs will quickly extend her front paws to the table and scarf the sandwich. I take responsibility for not doing a better job in the canine table manners training department, and I am working on it with them. When I catch the offending sandwich snatcher, I will reprimand her. Because she doesn't like my tone of voice, she may hang her head in the appearance of contrition, but she is not transformed. She has no sense of how losing the sandwich makes me feel. She is compliant to my response because she doesn't like the consequences, which is as much as a dog can do.

You and the other humans in your life are capable of much more. If a primary concern in your relationships is an authentic responsiveness to how you impact each other, you will have a pretty good life. Note that I don't mean responsiveness in the sense of an overly responsible codependent: "Am I making everyone happy? Everyone's happiness is my responsibility, and when someone is unhappy, I caused that." That is not what we're going for. There is a big difference between caring about how you impact someone and taking full responsibility for the other person's feelings and happiness in life. You are an influence, and those in your life influence you. Influence doesn't connote ownership.

We matter to each other. We make a difference to each other. People who care about their impact on another person, for good or for bad, are following the Golden Rule: "So in everything, do to others what you would have them do to you, for this sums up the Law and the Prophets" (Matthew 7:12). Look at how you affect others and how they affect you. This will help you determine if a relationship is one with a good future for vulnerability and going beyond boundaries.

14

Is This Person (Really) Connected to Good People?

I recently spoke at a workshop for parents of school-age kids. Our son Ricky attended college in the same city where I was speaking, so I asked him to address the group for a few minutes. I wanted him to give them the perspective of their child ten years into the future. During his comments, Ricky mentioned the important role athletic coaches played in his own childhood development. "The coaches were always yelling the same things at me that my parents were saying," he said. He wasn't trying to get sympathy. His point was that the values and behaviors expected of him at home were reinforced by other sources. In other words, he received integrated and consistent messages about what was expected of him.

Ricky's childhood experience of consistent messaging demonstrates a critical piece of what makes a person someone with whom it's okay to take a relational risk. It's safe to take a risk with people who are *connected (really connected) to some good people.* They don't have to have perfect friends in their lives, but they must be connected to people who are good for them and who are helping them become a better person—the kind of individual who will in turn help you to become a better person as well.

People hang around certain people for a reason. They may "fall in" with others in a random fashion, but they don't stay with them for a random reason. And you can understand a great deal—both good news and bad—about people by the friends they keep: "Bad company corrupts good character" (1 Corinthians 15:33). By inference, the reverse is also true: good company helps develop good character. You want the person to whom you become close to be surrounded by those who live out the biblical instruction to "spur one another on toward love and good deeds" (Hebrews 10:24).

Earlier, I stressed the importance of being with the right people and how most of the significant parts of life concern relationship. So it's not much of a leap to see the significance of this when you are trying to determine whether it's worth taking risks to move deeper into intimacy with someone. Think how difficult life has been when you did not have the right people around you: how weak you were, how distorted your thinking was, or how unable you were to make the choices you needed to make.

For example, Paul, a friend of mine, went through a difficult time when he was in his twenties. He moved to a new city for a job. He wasn't around his old support system, and he wasn't connecting to some good people in the new place. He ended up overdoing it on the party scene, developing a drinking problem, and actually getting engaged out of the blue to the wrong woman. It took him a long time and a lot of misery to get his life back on course. He simply did not have the right people around him to give him the stability he needed.

In the same way, if the person with whom you are preparing to risk has no sustaining and healthy relationships, you are putting yourself in jeopardy. You are drinking from a well that may not have much to offer.

Why You Need People Who Are Connected to Good People

There are two overriding reasons why anyone with whom you may want to move beyond boundaries needs to be connected to a good group of people: the other person needs a source of support as well as a source of truth that does not depend on you.

A good way to understand this is to look at the idea of open and closed systems. A closed system is an organization (or a person) that has no input from the outside world. It is entirely dependent on itself. An open system interacts with other organizations and people, receiving energy, support, and resources from the outside. In that way, those you relate to need to be open systems, getting good things from other people besides yourself.

The Other Person Needs a Source of Support That Does Not Depend on You

In any healthy relationship, people give grace and support to each other. They are interested in each other, draw one another out, are safe, and provide empathy. You come away from an encounter with the other person feeling more alive, refreshed, loved, and ready to take on the challenges of life. The way to ensure that this process works right is for both of you to have sources of support besides each other. Then, if one of you occasionally has an empty tank, there are places for the other person to go. If you have a disagreement and are alienated, you have other people to help you make the next move.

For example, when Barbi and I were dating, we spent a lot of our time with her friends and my friends. We lived in different cities and weren't from the same relational circles, so we double-dated with her friends and mine. We discovered that we liked each other's closest friends a great deal. This was a major factor in our decision to move ahead in the relationship. I knew she had individuals who were full of grace around her and to whom she was vulnerable. I had the same. We were surrounded by those who were for us and who were willing to know us at a deep level.

Avoid unhealthy dependence. When such relationships are not in place, you run the risk of entering an unhealthily dependent relationship with the person. Dependence itself is normal and something God intends for us. We need love and care from each other just as we need love and care from God. But unhealthy dependence occurs when the person's connectedness rises and falls with how much and how well you are providing for his or her relational needs. It is similar to a parent-child relationship. A small child has friends she depends on for companionship and support. But she has a focused and intense dependence on her parents. They are her life-support system.

My friend Shandra has an adult son, and their relationship has been tough for a long time. As a teenager, he got in with the wrong crowd and developed alcohol and drug problems. He's now a young adult and still struggles with his addictions. As often happens, he occasionally straightens things out for a few months and says he's committed to getting help and getting healthy. But then he inevitably hangs out with the wrong crowd and ends up in trouble again.

You can imagine how this has impacted Shandra over the years. She has experienced pain from his rejections, hurt for his state, and guilt about the role her own weaknesses and failures may have played in his condition. However, at this point, she has a different issue. She would like an adult-to-adult friendship with her son. She doesn't want to mother him or take care of him; she just wants to be closer to him. This is how God designed us to relate; it's part of the leaving and cleaving process. When children grow up to be adults, they and their parents enter into more of a mutual friendship while still maintaining the respect and honor due a parent.

But Shandra can't do that. Every time she tries to establish a two-way, mutual friendship, things go well for a bit, but then they break down again. For example, they meet for dinner, and she takes a risk to share something about her own life. Her son listens, engages, and is actually there for her. But sooner or later, he reverts to his old relationships. As his life once again spirals downward, he relates to her in toxic ways —he is combative, provokes fights, or accuses her of being controlling. Or, on the other end of the spectrum, he may become dependent and want her to solve his problems. She wants to go beyond boundaries with him, but this is not the right season.

When she asked me for guidance, I said, "I wouldn't revisit this with him until he has spent significant and structured time with both healing environments and with good friends for a minimum of a year." This sounded like a long time to her, but she has stuck to my recommendation.

So far, he has not been able to maintain contact with a counselor, support group, or healthy friends for longer than three months, and the clock starts over again after each relapse. But this is the best thing Shandra can do for herself, and for him, until he is willing to let the right people in. Shandra is committed to being as healthy as she can be for her son.

Her hope and plan is that, once he has connected on a deeper and more regular level with those who can help him, the dependencies in those relationships will be resolved. When that happens, he will be free to relate to her on a more mature and mutual level. It is a lose-lose situation to be around an adult child who is still going through his dependence-independence struggles, with you as the target.

It's initially exciting and maybe a little flattering to have someone say that you are all he or she needs to get by. You may even have to come to terms with your own codependency, your "need to be needed." But in the long run, if you truly are all this person needs to get by, you can have a mess on your hands — ranging from feeling drained and like a pseudo-parent to, in extreme cases, stalking problems. You just don't want these sorts of dynamics.

Don't assume church attendance qualifies. Sometimes Christians make the assumption that if the person is attending church, they can relax and assume he or she is living in community and is connected to good people. But let's take a closer look at that assumption.

For Christians, church is a given. Church is where Christians connect with God and each other. It is necessary and vital. Unfortunately, however, we can't assume that everyone in a church is relationally safe and healthy — just as we can't assume that everyone who doesn't go to church is relationally dangerous and unhealthy. Both camps have both sorts. That is why Henry Cloud and I wrote *Safe People* — to help people see that good character is about more than merely having faith in God.[8]

The only way to know for sure is to spend time with the church people your friend is spending time with. In addition to living according to the Bible, are they also real and authentic people? Or are they disconnected and detached from real life, stuck in a black-and-white or intellectualized faith? Can they connect on a deep level? Do they extend and receive grace? Do they appear to be individuals who can fill up your friend's gas tank when you can't? You want to be around those who live out the entire Bible, not just the abstracts. Christians can be full of joy and peace and also be vulnerable and authentic at the same time.

Take advantage of the open system that provides grace and relational support to those in your own life. You will be more graced by those people in turn. But there is another aspect as well, and that has to do with the truth.

The Other Person Needs a Source of Truth That Does Not Depend on You

It is vital that the person with whom you are considering having a relationship not only receives grace and support from others, but also gets a healthy dose of reality and truth from them. This is the "yelling coach" part that my son Ricky spoke of. You know this is happening when the person exposes his life to people who love him enough to tell him the truth. If he voluntarily hangs out with people who give him honest feedback and want him to grow, it's a good indication that he is capable of being a healthy influence on you.

A business friend of mine named Olivia is married to a man who tends to see things the way I do—more than the way she and I see things. We will be working together on a project, and I will give her some feedback like, "I think you might be missing the cost issues in your excitement about the potential of this project. I wish you'd be a little more frugal in making the business plan." She will look at me and say, "Have you and my husband been talking? He says the same thing." I cannot tell you how glad I am that Olivia's husband also watches his pennies — and provides her with another source of truth about her blind spots when it comes to money. It helps her and me both.

Think about the person you're interested in becoming close to. Do you want to be the one and only person in her life who is telling her the truth? Don't you think that would end up being frustrating and somewhat lonely? You are much better off when the individual is listening to a chorus of truth-telling people. The more good people there are giving input — in both of your lives — the better off everyone will be.

Here's one more aspect of this to consider. If you are a lone voice crying in the wilderness, you are likely to be negated. That is, the words of one person who is telling a painful or confrontive truth are often more readily dismissed by the other person. Even if you have the facts, evidence, logic, wisdom, and scriptural support on your side, the person will find ways to disregard what you are saying.

This dynamic has its roots in early childhood development. Kids are designed to leave their parents when they mature. Part of the growth process that prepares them for that separation is challenging their parents' points of view, opinions, and rules. Ultimately, the child uses those challenges to form her own beliefs and values and to establish an adult life.

However, this developmental process can sometimes go wrong. The child may be harshly criticized for challenging.

Or, her parents may repeatedly give in to her challenges, allowing her to win battles she should lose. As a result, she fails to develop the skills to accept feedback. Either way, she becomes resistant to hearing confrontation from anyone and interprets any truth telling as unloving or controlling. So she gravitates toward nice, loving, supportive friends who don't like to tell hard truths. She literally lives in a state of suspended development and goes through life that way.

Then, suppose you come along, fall in love with, and marry this person. In the course of the relationship, you notice an issue that bothers you. You say, "Sometimes you jump all over me when I forget to bring home the milk. I know I forget stuff, but can you be nicer when I make little mistakes?" And instead of saying, "Sorry, I do make a big deal of that; I'll try to do better," which would solve the problem, she says, "No one has ever said that to me, and you are overreacting and trying to be critical of me." And you think to yourself, "What just happened?"

What just happened is that your interaction triggered the old parent problem. You confronted her, and she interpreted your challenge as a parent who wants to change and control her. You have been negated. When this occurs in a marriage, couples counseling can be helpful to enable both people to recognize what's really going on.

I once worked with Sam and Janice, a couple who struggled to communicate. Sam had a way of turning anything his wife said about her own experience into something about his own experience. For example, instead of saying, "I didn't know that coming in late from work so much made you feel unloved," he would say, "I guess I'm never good enough for you." "That's not it," Janice would say, "I just want you to hear me. You keep turning what I say about how I feel into a statement about how I make *you* feel instead." "No, I don't," he'd retort. "There you go again putting me down."

When I had seen him do this several times myself, I said, "Sam, you have a tendency to turn Janice's experiences around and make them statements about you." I gave him a couple of examples. "You know, I never thought about it that way," he said, "That's true, I do do that." Janice almost jumped off the couch: "What? I've said this a million times!"

Sam was genuinely confused and didn't think he had ever heard this feedback before. It took us awhile, but Janice was finally able to see the negation as something Sam did that had more to do with him than it did with her. Eventually, she could laugh about it, though the laughing part took a little longer.

This story illustrates how important it is that your potentially important individual be grounded in loving and honest relationships. Other people can be your "yelling coaches," people whose honest feedback reinforces your feedback and diminishes the risk that you will be negated. Within that larger relational context, the other person does not relate to you as a parent to reject, but as a person he or she cares about and wants to respond to. That is why we all need several people in our lives who are honest with us and routinely practice "speaking the truth in love" (Ephesians 4:15).

The open system is important. Make sure anyone you find significant for yourself is connected to regular and healthy sources of grace and truth. Get to know these other people. Find out what she is learning and experiencing with them. You are creating an environment for relational growth for both you and her.

There are ways to see what you need to see in the other person. They are in this next section.

Five Indications the Other Person Is (Really) Connected to Good People

If the person has great relationships outside of yours, there will be evidence in his life of this. Remember that health attracts health, and there will be observable indications that this is happening. Here are some signs to help you see how connected the person is to the right kind of relationships. These five indicators aren't always apparent right away, but they will be over time.

You Share Similar Healthy Values with Them

As you get to know the "good people" in the other person's relational network, you sense that, in broad strokes, you share the same values. Like you, they value God, relationship, honesty, responsibility, and authenticity. This is not a checklist; the other people may not even use those words or have put much thought into what their values are. But these values emerge in their conversations and how they relate to each other and to you. You don't have to expect them to be perfect, but you need to know that they are basically good people whose lives and relationships give evidence that they care about the right things.

Allow some margin here. Your potential relationship and his or her friends may not have the same background you have and may not be intentional about relational and growth issues. For example, if you talk about your small group, they may not know what you are talking about. Of course, you yourself may not know what that term means either! Actually, that reinforces the point here. People can have good values but different contexts and opportunities, so don't rule them out if they haven't been to the same clubs you belong to, so to speak.

Suppose, for example, that your potential relationship's best friends have never read a personal-growth book or been to a relationship seminar (again, you might not have either, but think of this for argument's sake). However, in conversation with them you bring up something you're struggling with, such as a problem with your parents or a conflict at work. If they move toward you and are understanding and supportive, that shows a value. If they change the subject or don't engage, that's not such a good sign. Don't be rigid about this, however. Don't write them off after one evening with a statement like, *We had dinner, and all they wanted to talk about was sports.* Give people an opportunity for their values to show up. Be yourself and see how you relate to them and how they relate to you.

You Like Them

You enjoy being with the friends of your potential person. You can see yourself spending time with them, and it's a pleasant thought. You don't have to force yourself to enjoy being with them, which never works anyway. The healthier a relationship is, the more likely it is that everyone's friends will like one another. This doesn't necessarily mean you'll all have common interests or personalities. It has more to do with character.

The healthier you are, the more drawn you are to other healthy people. If you have one set of friends that does not get along at all with another set of friends, that may possibly reflect some conflicts in you. For example, suppose you have a crazy impulsive side of you, but also an uptight, guilty part. The two parts are not very integrated, and you may find yourself being out of control, but then swinging to the extreme of self-judgment and compulsivity. You may have friends who relate to one of these swings, but not the other. They may not get along, because they reflect your own conflict inside.

That also applies to the person you are interested in. For example, your friends may be more conservative in lifestyle, while his may be a little more casual. But do you like them? People who can only be comfortable with those who are similar to them most likely have a psychological issue. They don't have enough grace inside them to appreciate differences, so they feel more secure with those who are like them. If you do find that it's hard to like his friends, first make sure that you aren't the problem.

You See Their Vulnerability in Relationships

Your potential person not only hangs out with the good people in her life, she also gets real with them. They know her dreams, her past, and her struggles. She lets them into her heart. I titled this chapter with "(really)" in it because there are surface friendships, and then there are really deep and vulnerable relationships. Most likely, the person you are considering, whether it be for love, friendship, reconciliation, or business, is not living as a hermit in a shack in the woods. He is probably around people and has a social life. You may know those people and feel comfortable that they are good folks. However, that doesn't mean that the person you're interested in is truly connected to them. Lots of people can slide through life being unknown or largely unknown. It happens all the time.

It is a simple enough matter to talk to her about her relationships, or to be with her when she is with them. Even if you don't meet them, if she is vulnerable to them, she will have something to say about how much they affect her. For example, "I went shopping with Elaine" is fine, but it doesn't tell you much. But "While I was shopping with Elaine, we talked about some of our own failures and how we could help support each other" is a much better picture.

You See Them Relate outside of You

Suppose you like these people and think that they are a good indicator the person you're interested in is, or is becoming, a healthy person. Does she spend time with these people because she knows it is important to you or because it is important to her? This is often the case when, for example, in dating or a troubled marriage, the person moving beyond boundaries (you) notices that the other person has no other really healthy connections. So you suggest some: a good church, a therapist, a small group, some of your friends. And the other person begins connecting with good people.

Make sure that he or she "gets the virus" of being with good people. Does he spend time with these folks, even if the event doesn't involve you? Can you tell that she is getting something out of these relationships, or does she provide reports of her time with them like a school kid shows a report card to a parent? You will find out in time, because the person either will or won't need reminding to spend time with them. And you will see that these good people do or do not matter to the person.

You See Good Fruit in Them

The person you're interested in should become a better person through his relationships with other people. And by better, I mean better—not just the same and not worse. I was working with a woman named Ellie whose husband, Connor, was very passive and disconnected from her. He was not a controlling man. In fact, he was just the opposite. He wanted her to be in charge: to take all the initiative to talk, to make the social calendar, and to make the financial decisions. She felt alone in the marriage because she had to be in charge of everything. But when she did take charge of things, he resented her and told her she was being controlling. She couldn't win.

Ellie set some boundaries with Connor, not for the purpose of leaving him, but in order to protect herself. For example, she spent time with friends and in activities that didn't involve him because he simply wanted to watch TV every evening without talking. It was a sad situation. At my suggestion, Ellie also asked him to join a men's group, where other guys could support him and encourage him to move beyond his passive role. Then, if it went well, she would drop her boundaries and reengage in the relationship.

Connor found a men's support group and attended for several months, but it backfired. Instead of stepping up to the plate and taking more initiative, he became more resentful of her and withdrew further. I am not exactly sure how it happened, but I think he didn't really show the other men who he was inside and instead spent most of his time asking the group to help him tolerate the pain of living with a controlling wife. In terms of the men's group, my guess is that they were just a bunch of nice guys who believed everything he said and didn't check out the realities.

Because the fruit of Connor's relationship with the group was not good, I recommended Ellie continue to keep some distance from him. Then he was resentful of me! Finally, he found another group that loved him, accepted him, and also told him the truth about his passivity and its effect on her. Things got better and the outcomes improved. In time, Ellie was able to move into a closer and more vulnerable relationship with Connor. That's what is supposed to happen when we are really connected to good people—we grow and become better people ourselves.

Let me paint the best blue-sky scenario. You have a strong support system. It may be informal, formal, or both. That is, you may just have some great friends with whom you do life, who love you, accept you, and help you be a better person. Or you may meet regularly with a vital small group that has a clear purpose and structure for learning and sharing. Or perhaps you have both.

These support systems are your fuel, what keeps you going down the path of relational health and success. The person with whom you are beginning or continuing a relationship has the same thing, but with different players. You can trust that he or she has other places to go for support and for good feedback, just as he or she can trust that you do. That is the scenario to shoot for. Your chances of success and developing the intimacy you seek will be much greater when you are (really) connected to good people.

15

Can This Person Handle a Relationship with You?

If you hope to enter a relationship with someone that will involve risk and vulnerability, you want to make sure that person can handle who you are. That is, any personal connection is easy to navigate when you put your best foot forward, such as bringing your strengths and relational gifts into the attachment. This persona constitutes someone who is not difficult to love. But vulnerability requires bringing parts of yourself to the light that are not so lovable at times: weakness, need, failure, and flaws. It is critical that the person be able to relate to and care about these aspects of you as well, as they are also an essential part of you.

You won't be at the top of your game every day. And you need to be able to not only acknowledge your own weaknesses but receive a helpful response to them as well. This might mean the person doesn't expect more of you than you're capable of when you are under stress. Or it might mean the person knows what your trigger points are and what sort of things hurt you and discourage you. Just as a bridge needs to be strong enough to carry the weight of the vehicles that cross it, anyone you commit to must be able to handle your "weight" as well. Just because you have weaknesses and failures doesn't mean that you are the worst, darkest, most dysfunctional person in the world. It doesn't mean you are living in a crisis right now. It just means that you, and everyone else who exists on the planet, have weight, and we all need help with that weight.

You Need to Need

You have needs, and you cannot meet them all on your own. You need someone to listen, to give in practical ways, to advise, and to help you with decisions. This is normal life. In order for your needs to be met, someone will have to invest time with and energy in you. Being vulnerable with someone places a demand on that person. They have to take time out of their busy schedule, put their own agenda on hold, and momentarily put their own experiences and feelings aside in order to be a friend to you. This is the weight of relationship. You bear the weight of those who are important to you, and they bear yours, willingly and cheerfully.

It helps to be aware of this: You can be a drain! That doesn't mean you are a high-maintenance person who sucks the life out of the world, which is a common fear of people who compulsively help others and forget themselves. It simply means you legitimately require certain amounts of grace and attention from others. Many people feel more naturally inclined to be in the giving role than the taking role. And it is true that being a giver is a great thing; "it is more blessed to give than to receive" (Acts 20:35). But we can't give what we haven't received in the first place. That's how God runs the universe. You get love, grace, and truth, and then you pass it along to others.

Anyone you are considering opening up to must be aware that you are going to cost them something. You may have great strengths, resources, and a deep well of compassion. These are good things. But at some point or another, you are going to be discouraged, empty, lonely, angry, frustrated, prickly, and dependent. You will require some care, and you may not even be that easy to love. Whomever you invest in must know what they are getting into.

So take a look at the person with whom you are considering going beyond boundaries. Does she have the emotional resources to handle you? Can he put his concerns on the back burner and enter your world? Or do you notice that the focus and energy tend toward her situation, in a way that neither party becomes aware of? This might be a person to love, help, support, and find resources for, but it may not be a person with whom you can move ahead in pursuing an intimate relationship.

Not everyone can handle you. This isn't an indictment of anyone. Sometimes it is just the wrong time or the wrong person. But you need a way to kick the tires and see if all of you will be okay with all of the other person. Here are some questions to ask as you get to know the person you are considering.

Are They in a Good Place Themselves?

It takes a certain amount of personal strength to provide love, grace, and support to another individual. As we've noted, relationship provides the fuel of life that keeps us going toward growth and our goals. When there is an authentic connection in a relationship, that means there is a transfer of fuel from one person to another. Anyone you are considering getting closer to must have the ability to provide that fuel.

A woman I know, I'll call her Angie, asked me to help her with a relationship she had with her sister Rachel. She wanted to get closer to Rachel, but every time they got together to talk, Rachel monopolized the conversation. This dynamic had been going on for several years. Rachel had had a tough life, including a bad divorce and major kid problems. She tended toward dependency and allowing people to control her. She did not have many close friends and lived an isolated life. You can see how this might add up to a one-way relationship with Angie, who, though she had also had some serious life challenges of her own, still worked on herself, had experienced a lot of growth, and was now in a pretty good spot in life.

As it worked out, Rachel's own brokenness dominated the relationship with her sister. When they talked, Rachel spent most of the time going over her loneliness, her issues with the ex, and her kids' struggles. She was a nice and kind person at heart, but she remained unaware that she was controlling the relationship. Her neediness simply poured out as an open fire hydrant gushes water. Rachel's isolation was so deep that her sister's natural warmth actually attracted the dependency.

This put Angie in a dilemma. She really wanted a more intimate relationship with Rachel, but every conversation they had ended with Angie not only feeling unheard, but drained as well. Still, Angie felt bad that she felt this way. She wanted to look forward to spending time with her sister.

The first thing I suggested was that she talk to Rachel about this, in as gentle a way as possible, something like, "I am so glad we are in each other's lives and you mean so much to me. But I do have a request. Sometimes when we talk, I have things going on in my life to tell you about, and we seem to never get to them. I want to be there for you, and I always will, but can we try a little time for me as well?"

I knew this was a risk for Angie. Her sister might feel attacked or blamed and turn away from the relationship. But, from what Angie had told me about Rachel, I thought Rachel seemed to be capable of hearing the spirit in which Angie was making her request.

So they had the talk. Rachel was surprised and a little embarrassed about the imbalance. She said she wanted a two-way relationship as well and agreed to work on that in their connection.

It worked at first. and then it stopped working. The first few phone calls and lunches were better. Rachel made sure she asked how Angie was doing, and Angie talked about her job or her marriage. Angie let Rachel know how much she appreciated the consideration. Then, gradually, Rachel's life issues began to take over the conversation again. Her major struggles were just too pressing for her to see beyond her pain and enter Angie's world. I told Angie to refer Rachel to a therapist, support groups, financial counselors, and mentors. She did that. Rachel has not really gotten the vision of personal growth yet. She tends to be passive and allows her troubles to overwhelm her. At the time of this writing, Angie has not been able to have a mutual, two-way relationship with Rachel. Perhaps, if Rachel commits to the healing she needs, that will happen in time.

The point here is that you need to see if the person is in a good spot to help you unpack life with them. She does not have to have a perfect life. She can even have big problems. But she must have enough bandwidth and energy left over from meeting her own demands of reality to be present and engaged with you. Do you find, as Angie did, that the focus drifts back on to the other person's situation most of the time? Or do you find that she stays interested, is emotionally there, and takes initiative to enter your world? This is a large part of what has to happen.

Is the Person Willing to Invest in the Relationship?

The person must be invested in you or be willing to be invested in your relationship. To invest is to devote a resource, in this case, one's love, attention, focus, time, and energy. Vulnerable relationships are not casual drive-by relationships, where "I'll see you when I can." Things are too fragile and important for that kind of breezy level of commitment. Healthy intimate relationships involve a dedication of one's self to the betterment of the other. You need someone who will count the cost of having an attachment to you and who is willing to then make a real commitment.

That does not mean, however, that there is something wrong with someone who doesn't want to make the investment. There may be some perfectly legitimate reason why you are not on his or her radar. If it's a dating relationship, as the best-selling book says, maybe "he's just not that into you." There is no bad guy in that sort of situation. It's a matter of preference and choice. The same goes for friendships. One person may just want to put more into the relationship than the other person.

In marriage. A marriage two people are trying to rebuild is a different matter. Making a marriage work as God intended it to work requires that both people be "all in." When this doesn't happen and one person is on the fence in the commitment, things can't really move forward. Your most vulnerable self simply cannot take the risk if the other person is not invested in the connection. In those sorts of scenarios, you must first address the lack of investment and commitment because, in a marriage, a lack of commitment isn't just a preference or a choice, it is a problem. Is he questioning if he wants to stay or go? Is she putting time and energy that should go into the marriage into work or her friends instead? We just can't open up and trust until the investment is in place.

I worked with a man named Tyler whose wife left him, moved in with another man, and had a child by that other man. Incredibly, Amelia didn't want to divorce her husband. She still had some feelings for him, primarily because he was a safe and stable figure in her life. So she stayed connected to him and made contact from time to time.

It was a terrible situation for Tyler. He loved Amelia and wanted to give her grace and be patient. And yet the realities were that she was deeply committed to another man with just the occasional bouts of missing him. Tyler's friends didn't understand why he put up with this and wouldn't divorce her. To them, the marriage was over, and he needed to move on. He himself didn't understand why he hung on either. As we dug deeper, however, we found that he had grown up in a troubled family. As a boy, he handled family problems by being the strong one, the patient one, and the one who looked at the positive aspects of the situation. For example, if his mom and dad fought, he tried to intervene and show them both points of view, as a marriage counselor would—but he was *seven years old*. He also hoped for the best, as kids do, for their deepest longing is that Mom and Dad stay together and love each other. Regrettably, his parents divorced.

When you combine Tyler's childhood role as mediator and his deep longing for an intact family, it's not surprising to see why he hung on to an incredibly painful situation for so long. He began to sift through the early character patterns, and that helped him to clarify what he needed to do in the nightmare scenario. Amelia could not truly invest in Tyler. She was not a person with whom he could be vulnerable. She was the wrong person to choose to move beyond boundaries with.

If you are in a marriage in which one person is not fully invested, you simply must have others you are connected with to support you. Your spouse is not yet the one to fully trust. It is to be hoped that this can change in time. But, while you are "for" her and love her, do not put yourself in emotional jeopardy by giving her all of yourself, until she can do that as well.

In families. In other relationships, such as with family members, a person sometimes expects a relational investment that is not there. A woman may wish her dad was more emotionally connected to her. He may not call or ask about her life or kids or visit, for example. It can be in the other direction as well, in which the parent of an adult child wishes for more of a relationship than that child wants to give. The ideal, of course, is for family members to love each other. Even after children grow up and leave home, family members can still be connected to each other and involved in each other's lives. The roles simply shift. Instead of parents being the source of life and provision for the children, they are all friends with a shared history who honor and love each other.

Within families, a lack of investment may be because of a rift. It could be that there is a disagreement that hasn't been settled, an unresolved character issue such as an emotional injury or a substance abuse problem that gets in the way. If these issues are not worked through, family members remain alienated, sometimes for decades.

When there is a rift or a self-absorption problem, do whatever you can do on your part to be as healthy as possible, to forgive, and to attempt to reconcile. If the other person is willing to look deep within and take ownership of his or her part, family members can often come closer together again.

There are times in families, however, when there is no alienation or no rift. The issue is simply that one person desires more of an investment than another person. No one is mad, no one is hurt, no one is cutting people off. There are just different levels of time, energy, and commitment. I don't see this as a good-guy/bad-guy issue. Most friendships aren't exactly the same in how much time each party wants to spend together, for example. In fact, though marriage is a total commitment, even spouses have differing needs for the amount of time they spend together. One person needs more space, another more togetherness, and that is a matter of love, adjustment, sacrifice, and negotiation. The same is often true in families when the kids are now adults, and everyone has different expectations about the level of their investment in the family.

The point is this: *moving beyond boundaries requires a commitment from both people.* Intimacy can't exist without that sort of safety. It's important to take a look at how invested the other person is in having a relationship with you and in knowing you deeper. As I've noted above, there may be a "no fault" reason that the person isn't invested. If so, accept it, be gracious, adjust to a less committed relationship, and look elsewhere. That's how adults navigate life, and this attitude will protect you as well.

Does the Person Have Good Character?

Does the person you are interested in have the internal character that bodes well for a healthy relationship? Relational investment is one thing and character is another. I define character as the ability to meet life's demands. Part of that ability includes being able to make a good connection. Character isn't about being perfect. If it were, you and I would be disqualified. But it is about having the stuff inside to take good care of the connections you have.

For example, I spoke with a woman on our radio show whose husband was an alcoholic. Among other things, he disappeared for long periods of time and was ruining the family finances. It got so bad that she had to ask him to leave the house. Her question was, "How do I know when to let him move back in?"

"What is he doing about the drinking?" I asked.

"He doesn't think he has a problem," she said. "He says I'm overreacting."

"If everything you are telling me is true, you aren't overreacting; you are being realistic. What do some objective people in your life say?"[9]

"My pastor, my therapist, and my small group all know him and agree that it's a really bad problem."

"Why would you consider allowing him to come back if he's in denial about his problem?"

"Because he misses me so much, and he loves me, and he's lonely."

"I understand that. People in denial can love and miss

someone. In fact, that's why you don't want to let him back in. That is your leverage for him to get help. If he didn't miss you, you'd have a bigger problem."

At this point, the conversation began to shift from him to her.

"But if he really loves me, I can't stand to be cutting him off," she said. In other words, the caller was now articulating her own longings and demonstrating her codependency, which was a large part of the issue.

"I know it's hard," I said, "and you need support from some people to stand firm. But look at it this way. Let's say you have a house rule that your kids don't go out to play with their friends until they do an hour of homework after school. That's a good rule. But today, your daughter wants to play with her friends and blows off the homework. She just doesn't want to do it. And you say she can't go out. She begs and pleads, and it's not like she wants to go do drugs. She wants to have some healthy, innocent fun time. What do you do?"

The caller was quiet for a moment and then said, "I get it."

One of the signs of character is that a person does what it takes to restore a relationship. If he is at fault, he apologizes, changes, stops drinking too much, asks forgiveness, gets pastoral help, gets in a growth group, gets in therapy, makes himself accountable to a financial planner, goes to a twelve-step group, or says to you, "Tell me what I need to do so I won't hurt you so much." Missing, longing, loneliness, and love are good things. They show a capacity for attachment, which helps. But they are not enough. Character says he has to do more than want you; he has to change to be a better person.

Love is not enough. Nor are attentiveness, romantic feelings, a charming personality, great competencies and skills, or promises to change. You need substance underneath the topping. Don't sell yourself short. Character always wins over time.

What's the Reality of Your Circumstances?

There are some practical realities that affect whether or not you should make yourself vulnerable and invest in a relationship. In that sense, investment and character are not enough either. Pay attention to the circumstances in which you both find yourselves. For example, consider the following situations:

- You want to go into business with someone, but he doesn't have the money or the sweat equity to hold up his end.

- You want to be closer to your spouse, but you have a child in a health crisis, and both of you must first devote your energies to that.

- You are interested in dating someone whose divorce is not final or who is recently divorced or who has not done any divorce recovery.

- You are interested in dating someone who is going through a financial and career crisis, and there is little time for a relationship.

- You would like to become closer friends with someone who will soon be moving from the area for a new job.

- You want to reconnect to a difficult family relationship, but it's the holidays, and everything is chaotic right now.

- You are in high school and in love, but you and the person you're interested in are planning to go to different colleges far away from each other.

You only have so much time, energy, and emotional wherewithal to put into a person. When circumstances are involved, there are no sides to take. There are just realities, and you must pay attention to them. You may be able to overcome some of these, or perhaps you should wait until a better season. You must factor in your circumstances. Don't ignore them. You aren't being cold-hearted or selfish. You can still be a loving, warm, people-oriented individual who has her head screwed on right.

Count the cost here. Relationships are one of the best things anyone can experience. But if you just buy some time to think through these matters, you are much more likely to come out with a winning connection with a person you won't later regret or need to recover from.

16

For Dating and Marriage: Does This Person Go Beyond Passion?

If you are considering moving beyond boundaries in a love relationship, either dating or marriage, this chapter addresses a specific and important aspect of romantic connection. It has to do with the capacity of the other individual to move beyond romance, passion, and sexuality. The reason for this is that, to some extent, we are afflicted by a Hollywood distortion about relationships.

Don't get me wrong—I'm not anti-Hollywood. I am a movie person, and my sons are in school studying film. But we need to free ourselves of a distortion embedded in the DNA of the movie culture: passion trumps everything. That is, if you deeply connect on a romantically passionate level, you have entered relational Nirvana, and your love conquers all. This is the stuff of lots of great entertainment, but it is not how real relationships actually go to the next level.

A good friend of mine, Sharon, was dating Alex, a man to whom she was extremely attracted. He had many of the qualities she looked for: the same spiritual values, warmth, lots of friends, and ambition, and it didn't hurt that he looked like a fashion model. Plus, he was an incurable romantic, and she loved that aspect of the relationship. Alex was the king of long nights, longing glances, flowers, endearing words, and great spots to have dinner. Sharon was smitten with this guy.

Then, reality reared its ugly head in the form of a tendency for Alex to be financially irresponsible. He was laid off from a job and wanted to crash at her place for a while. He borrowed money and didn't repay it. Sharon thought she could solve the problem with a direct conversation. She told him that although she loved him, she really needed him to get his own place and pay her back or get on a regular payment plan. She needed to see some sign of fiscal responsibility.

Alex responded by evading the questions, telling her how attractive she was and how he wanted to take her to a great dinner and spend quality time with her. She was a little taken aback, because nothing he said corresponded to her statements. She tried again. This time he said he wanted to give her a massage! Finally, Sharon realized that Alex was not capable of dealing with reality and ended the conversation. It's not surprising that she also ended the dating relationship shortly thereafter.

Though this sounds like an extreme example, it illustrates that some people can only relate to the opposite sex in the romantic or sexual arena. It's as if they learned their entire repertoire on reality TV. An abundance of passion can certainly be attractive in the right context, but if there is nothing that goes beyond passion, such an individual is not ready for a relationship with you.

Passion's Place

Romantic passion is a wonderful thing. It has energy and draws a couple closer. It is physical, sensual, emotional, and full of life: "Let him kiss me with the kisses of his mouth —for your love is more delightful than wine" (Song of Songs 1:2). In the best long-term marriages, passion plays a strong role throughout the decades. Two people experience all the levels of relationship that are possible: shared values, friendship, spiritual connections, vulnerabilities, and passion. Each aspect is woven into the tapestry of the complete connection.

Passion has its own special place and usefulness in the relationship; it helps a man and a woman feel extremely close to each other, as sexual attraction temporarily diminishes the boundaries that separate two people. In the sexual embrace, each person feels a deep oneness with the other. It is pleasurable in and of itself and brings a great deal of intensely positive feelings into the relationship. It is part of the process of having children and families. And it is a symbol of how strong God's love is for us as well, since he sees us as his bride: "Therefore I am now going to allure her; I will lead her into the wilderness and speak tenderly to her" (Hosea 2:14). We can then learn much about our relationship with God by understanding and experiencing passion.

The benefit of passion is that it provides a buffer when reality emerges, and the couple finally has to face up to each other's flaws. They may be minor, moderate, or major, but they are imperfections, issues, and sins that will not go quickly away. They are hard to live with, and they cause relational problems. But the buildup of the relational equity, the goodwill, and the positive affection will help smooth over the rough spots while the couple wrestles with adapting to and integrating the less pleasant realities. Mature love then develops, in which each person knows the good and bad of the other and loves the entire person anyway.

Couples who understand passion from a mature perspective get it all. They win the lottery. They are able to have great sexual experiences. And they are also able to move into great vulnerability and openness to each other that go deeper than passion. *They don't really give up anything.* No couple with that sort of relationship would trade it for anything else. What can compare with an evening in which you share a fear or a need and receive deep empathy and understanding from your spouse as he safely explores who you really are at your core, followed by passion? These are some of the peak experiences shared by growing couples who do life right. And that's the place of passion.

When Passion Dominates

The problem comes when passion and romance are taken out of their place. Things go wrong in the same way that things go wrong when dessert is the entrée of the meal. There is no substance and no character to hold the relationship together. The two people feel disconnected, alienated, misunderstood, bored, or addicted. And they fail to grow together as two adults. When passion dominates a relationship, you will notice three trends that you need to be aware of. They don't mean that the relationship should end. They do mean, however, that the relationship should change and become less passion-based, before you move beyond boundaries.

Disappointment in Reality

When the initial and strongest passion begins to ebb and

reality is front and center, an individual can be disappointed in where it looks like the relationship is going. He or she may compare it to a former relationship and find that it fails: it is not as intense, as emotional, as fiery. The present relationship seems bland and even less connected and intimate. Rather than seeing the change as a potential invitation to move into even deeper vulnerability, it's viewed as going backward.

I was working with Scott, a single man who was dating Carol, a woman who loved romance and, with the same intensity, hated reality. He was always on the ropes with her, not knowing what to expect. They would have memorable moments and evenings, and Scott was sure she was the one. No one had ever made him feel as alive as Carol did.

But then, on those weekends when he would just want to hang out and watch TV with her or when he didn't have anything special planned, she grew restless and withdrew from him. When he talked about his financial problems or his fears of losing his job, Carol withdrew even more. She didn't like to have these sorts of conversations. She wanted him to "live for the moment, as that is all any of us have," as she put it. When Scott asked her about her own struggles, she shut down. Carol was perpetually disappointed in reality and did not want him to face his own realities, much less hers.

Scott tried to keep Carol interested. He did his best. He spent far too much money and energy on evenings and weekends to help her escape. Finally, however, he was not enough for her, and the relationship ended. He was devastated, for he truly cared about her. But over time, as we conducted the postmortem on their connection, he realized he had wanted her so much that he ignored her adversarial relationship with reality. Scott was ultimately better off that she ended the relationship, for he would likely have been engaged in a futile life of constantly trying to keep reality at bay on her behalf.

For yourself, then, look at what happens when there is no passion in your time together. Can he or she relate? Talk about normal life? Maintain interest in your normal activities? Be sure to pay attention to how connected to reality the person is.

Failure to Have Intimacy

In a marriage, one spouse often equates closeness with sex. That is, sexual relations serve as a shortcut to intimacy. While this is more typically a problem for men, women can also have the issue. There are some commonalities between closeness and sex, for example, such as loving feelings, moving toward the other person, and wanting to exclude others from their private world. The commonalities make it easy for a person to sometimes miss the differences between closeness and sex. This can cause great damage to a marriage. A wife will feel unloved and used. In his turn, her husband will feel her withdrawal and experience it as rejection. Then the two escalate in their alienation from each other.

I was talking to a man at a professional conference who asked me for some advice on his sex life. He said, "My wife isn't as sexual as I am, and she doesn't want to have relations as frequently as I do."

"Well, no couple has exactly the same level of desire," I said, "So that's not really a problem. Where is the problem as you experience it?"

"She doesn't seem as into it as I am when we are having sex. Like she's not really enjoying it."

"Yes, that does sound like a problem. So, she never has the degree of desire you do?"

"No, I don't think so."

"Have you asked her about this?"

"Yes. She says she loves me, and she knows it's important for me, so she doesn't mind."

"I think you guys can do better than that."

"How?"

"When you have relations, what do you do beforehand?"

"We put the kids to bed and we go to bed ourselves."

"Before you get actively sexual, do you hold her and ask her how she's feeling about her day and how she feels about you two?"

"No, not really."

I waited a beat and said, "So what do you think?"

"Now that I think about it," he said, "she always brightens up when I ask her how she's doing. But I just assume that if she doesn't bring something up, she's okay."

"It's pretty common for men to think that," I said. "But part of love is reaching inside your wife emotionally and finding out what's going on in her."

Then I referred him to Solomon: "The purposes of a person's heart are deep waters, but one who has insight draws them out" (Proverbs 20:5). This is true about a woman's heart as well. "Try that and let me know how it goes," I said. I felt reasonably sure things would get better, because I've seen this work many, many times.

The order of matters is this: listen and talk at a deeper level first, and put sex second. Especially for women, who are often relationally ahead of men, being heard and understood makes women feel loved and safe and opens the door to their own passion and desire. In this way, both the husband and the wife learn how to connect with each other, learn how to put the other person first, learn to value patience and relationship, and then experience sexuality as a result. There is certainly a place in a healthy marriage for more recreational and spontaneous sex. But make sure that, in the main, emotional intimacy trumps sexual intimacy.

Sometimes a spouse will think that sexuality is best enhanced by techniques and environment. He dims the lights, plays evocative music, massages her with scented oils, and wears sensual clothing. Those things can add to the experience. But I can't even count the women who tell me that all of these added up to very little in terms of increasing their own passion. It was the listening and the interest in her world that made the difference. There is no shortcut to connection. It takes time, effort, and the ability to put yourself second.

So assess whether you feel your spouse can enter into intimacy on the high road, not the shortcut. It could be, like the man I met at the conference, that your partner may truly not know the difference. So extend grace and communicate about what you need in the connection in order to feel sexual. Help your partner understand this.[10] But if your spouse resists this part, it's not a good sign that he or she can go beyond passion and sex with you. If the man at the conference had said to me, "She just needs to understand I'm wired this way and be more enthusiastic as a way of telling me she loves me," that would have been a red flag. He didn't. He has a good chance of going beyond boundaries with his wife. And you need to pay attention to the response you get as well.

Concern, Not Celebration, from Friends

In dating, one of the most abrupt wake-up calls about a person's ability to move beyond passion is to include the person in your friendships. Unless you have extremely codependent friends, they'll give you an earful of reality, and it will help you. If you hear something like, "You change when he's around; you're not like yourself the way you usually are with us," or "She's a nice person, but I couldn't find anything to talk about with her," or "He was just into you, and he really had no interest in anybody else," that is something to pay attention to. In the early stages of dating, a couple often wrap themselves in a bubble of absorption with only each other, in a world of their own. Let your friends help you see if there is a correspondence between that world and the real world. Instead of the comments I just described, a great report card would be something like, "He fits right in," or "I could tell she made an effort to connect with us," or "I'd like him even if he wasn't dating you" (you may have to worry about that last comment).

Distinguish between Romantic Language and Vulnerable Language

There is romantic language and there is vulnerable language. They are related, but different. Here are some examples of romantic language:

- You are so amazing.
- You are incredibly attractive.
- I want you so much.
- I've never felt like this with anyone (on the first date!).
- I feel like I've known you all my life (same).
- I could be like this with you forever.

These are perfectly fine romantic and passionate statements. They fit when two people are very attracted to each other. But you had better make sure you hear the following statements just as often:

- How are you?
- Tell me more about that.
- How did the boss make you feel when he said that?
- Did I hurt your feelings when I did that?
- How are you and I doing?
- I've struggled as well.

An intimate and passionate relationship *requires interest in the inner life of the person.* That inner life is not always full of passion, because not all of life is romantic. The person must have a full-orbed connection to all the deeper parts of you.

A Challenge to Women

Generally speaking, just as men tend to have an affinity for the more aggressive aspects of life, women tend to have a natural bent toward relationship. We men do need to work harder on connecting at deeper levels, and we can "go there," if we pay attention to this dimension of love. However, let me challenge the women here as well.

While your man is responsible to learn and grow in this area, *you are also responsible to let him know how important this is to you.* Sometimes, when a man only wants to relate on a romantic level or has little experience in true closeness, a woman becomes discouraged and resigned to this limitation in the relationship. She thinks, *That's just how men are—at least he has other good qualities.* Don't settle!

God designed both of you for intimacy. Your spouse is a better man for relating on vulnerable levels, just as you are a better woman for the same reasons. And the relationship is also a more mature and healthy one. I often tell a wife, for example, to say, "I do love you and want great sexual closeness with us. But I need to know that you care and want to know me as well. I will be much more responsive to you if you will do that with me." A good man will be touched by this, and the ones who are not have a real problem. You're not taking ownership of his issue; rather, you are taking ownership of your role in helping the relationship go deeper.

If you want to go beyond boundaries, you must also go beyond passion. Romance is the cart, not the horse. Vulnerability is the horse.

17

Is the Big Problem Being Solved the Right Way?

If you want to give an existing relationship a second chance, this chapter is for you. When you've been let down by someone who matters a great deal to you, moving beyond boundaries is not easy work—but it is important. If you are willing to risk and try again, good for you. Unless you are seriously codependent, your willingness means you have the sort of character that walks the second mile with someone. And that is a good thing.

At the same time, it's important that you think this through clearly. Your heart may be in the right place, for it is never wrong to care about someone. But, risk or no risk, *you are always the guardian of your heart.* As the steward of your one and only life, it is your responsibility—to God and to yourself—to be vulnerable when it is safe to do so. To open yourself up to a person who has shown no sign that things will be different is to jeopardize yourself. One of the most important things you can do in this regard is to figure out if the problem that was previously an obstacle is truly being transformed. In other words, is this person really changing? Is the big problem being solved the right way?

Here's an example. I worked with a couple in which the husband, Bill, was a nice guy but irresponsible. He was one of those likeable people who loves to hang out with others and is a lot of fun. But Bill's performance in life did not match up to his personality, especially in the area of finances and spending. He overspent on cars, gadgets, and entertainment. He also hid his spending habits, which meant his wife, Pam, was routinely surprised by huge credit card bills. These patterns took a major toll on the marriage. Pam was terrified of an uncertain financial future with him. She was not perfect and had her own issues as well, but his behavior came close to breaking up the marriage.

In our work together, Pam was clear that though she still loved Bill, she had lost all trust in him. She could not believe anything he said. "If he told me at noon that the sun was shining, I would go outside to check," she said. As is common in these situations, Bill did not want to acknowledge the severity of the problem or make the necessary changes. He wanted Pam to change, to stop blaming him, and to learn to trust him. "If you would be nicer to me and trust me," he said, "I would feel more supported, and I'd do better in my career."

I had to step in there and say, "You are right; she shouldn't be mean to you or attack you. But I don't want her to trust you."

Bill was bothered by that and said, "Don't you want the marriage to work out?"

"Sure I do," I said. "I want Pam to love you with no strings attached. But that is different from trust. While love is free, trust is earned. In the area of financial responsibility, I don't want her to relax and trust you until we have evidence that you have changed."

Again, Bill didn't like that: "You're both judging me," he said.

"No," I said, "neither of us is consigning you to hell. There is no judgment in this office. But you have not shown that you understand how deeply you have hurt her, nor have you made the necessary changes so that she can trust you again. If you and I were neighbors and I borrowed your screwdriver and didn't return it, then borrowed your saw and didn't return it, then your pliers and didn't return them, what would you do if I asked to borrow your hammer?"

"Of course I wouldn't lend it to you," he said. "Okay, I see the point."

Bill wasn't as sorry as I wanted him to be at that point. He still didn't seem to be able to acknowledge the impact he had on his wife, but it was progress.

"Here's the deal," I said. "I want you to submit your finances to Pam on a monthly basis for a year. She is in charge. You get an allowance. You both see a financial planner together. And we'll see, month by month, if you are really changing for her sake and the relationship's sake."

I turned to Pam: "If he does what I am asking, would you be open to trusting him again?"

"I would," she replied. "I want to get all this behind us. But it has to be real."

They agreed to the plan. Bill did some blaming at first, which happens frequently. But he humbled himself and allowed her to be in charge of the money. It wasn't easy, and there were some bumps, but by month four, Pam said to me, "I think I'm ready to trust him again. Let's let go of the plan; I want him to feel like he has his freedom again."

"I'm willing to compromise from a year to six months," I said, "but not down to four. Let's stay on the plan another sixty days."

As it turned out, Bill did fine. And Pam was able to get past her hurt and mistrust, because he had truly changed.

Hurt and mistrust are nothing more than signals. They tell you that you either have some healing to do, or the other person has some changing to do — or both. It's important to remember both sides of the equation, the "you" side and the "other person" side. If you don't heal, as we talked about in part 2, you won't ever be able to trust anyone. When the trust muscle is torn, it won't operate — no matter how safe or right the other person is. If the other person isn't trustworthy, your trust can direct you into some blind alleys. So, while monitoring if you are learning to trust again, also monitor how the other person is doing in the arena that caused a break in trust in the first place.

Evidence of Authentic Transformation

You need to see evidence of authentic transformation in order to move beyond boundaries with someone who has hurt you. That may seem like a difficult thing to assess, but there are at least four key pieces of evidence that characterize real heart change, all of which are observable — confession, ownership, remorse, and changed behavior. The degree to which these things are evident — or absent — is the degree to which you can feel safe about trusting this individual again.

Confession

Confession is agreement with the truth. Simply put, the person must agree that she has behaved in a way that has caused you distress. Confession is about reality, not perception. Something she did had a negative effect on you, and she and you agree on that. Confession provides a way for people to begin to reconnect as they acknowledge and agree about the truth of what has happened between them.

There are two parts to confession—agreement about what was done and agreement that it affected you. That is what you need to hear from someone with whom you want to move beyond boundaries. If she simply agrees that the behavior happened but fails to acknowledge that it impacted you, you don't have the kind of full confession that allows you to move on with each other.

I was consulting with a company beset by relational problems at the executive level. Among other things, I found that the president had lost touch with those who reported to her. Her tendency to be abrupt and direct came across to her colleagues as harsh and critical. She had alienated the people she supervised, and some of her top talent was close to quitting. The issue that kept her from solving that problem was a lack of full confession of how her harshness affected others.

I coached her on how to make better connections and on learning to admit when she was too brutal with them. I thought we were making progress, but we encountered a speed bump when I heard that she had done it again to a direct report. She had flayed him about a tactical error he had made in the company strategy, and she had done it in front of several of his colleagues. He was humiliated. I told her, "You have to change this. Go to him and apologize. You're the leader here." Her response was disappointing: "It's not that bad; he needs to have a thicker skin."

That is sometimes true, but not in this case. Her direct reports had pretty thick hides. She had no idea how deeply she demoralized these people. I had to be blunt with her, and though it took a while, she began to acknowledge the impact her behavior had on them. But it didn't happen until we talked about the relationship she had with her own cold and critical mother, who deeply wounded her and whose impact she had never fully dealt with. As a young adult, she simply left home and moved on, never knowing that she was repeating the relational dynamic she experienced with her mom. That understanding, and remembering how her mom's behavior had affected her, helped her soften up with others.

When the other person confesses, look for both admission of the truth and for acknowledgment that the behavior impacted you:

- I have been drinking too much and I know it scares you.

- I have been withdrawn and I know you feel lonely.

- I have been too angry and I know it has hurt your feelings.

- I have given you mixed messages about our relationship and I know you are confused.

- I have not been forthcoming with the truth and I know you can't trust me.

Keep both sides of the equation in mind; if they are not there, explain why they are important to you and to the relationship. Help the person to do both. Most reasonably healthy people can pull this off.

Ownership

To own a behavior is to take responsibility for it, without blame or excuse. When you own something, you are saying, "This is my problem and no one else's." If the person in your life owns his or her behavior, that's an encouraging sign. It feels good when someone owns what he's done; it makes you feel safer. In fact, you *are* safer because the person isn't disregarding his or her behavior. You can relax a bit and come closer. When the other person blames external forces, including you, for her behavior, she is effectively saying: *I am not really responsible for what I did, and therefore whatever really caused it could drive me to do it again. Watch out for me; I'm not in control of this.*

Take a look at the paired statements that follow for more examples of what it means when someone takes, or fails to take, ownership:

Ownership: My drinking is a problem.
No ownership: I need some stress relief from my work.

Ownership: I withdraw and isolate myself from you. Though there are reasons for it, it's my problem.
No ownership: I have to pull away because you are hard to live with.

Ownership: I blow up in anger when I shouldn't and I need to work on this.
No ownership: You push me too far.

Ownership: I give you mixed messages, and they are a reflection of my own confusion inside.
No ownership: You want too much from me.

Ownership: I have been lying to you, and I have chosen that.
No ownership: Your lack of support makes me hide the truth.

Certainly, you may have made things more difficult because of your own issues, and you must always acknowledge those and work on changing them. But, even though you contribute to the relational problem, *you do not cause hurtful behavior.* Look for ownership instead of excuses or blame. Ask for it. Educate the other person about what it means to own her behavior and don't settle for less.

Remorse

Remorse is a good sign. It is a deep regret for what the remorseful person has done to you. Expressing remorse demonstrates love and care and affirms that your experience is important to the person even if in facing up to it, it is uncomfortable. It indicates that the person has the capacity to temporarily set aside his or her own reality and feel empathy for what has happened to you. You need to feel remorse for what you do to others, just as it is helpful for you to receive it as well from others.

Remorseful feelings are not guilt feelings, though they are often confused for each other. The emotion of guilt is a self-condemnation for a wrong done. It is self-oriented and self-attacking. It is more about the person's internal world than about his or her compassion for you. Imagine that someone important to you has mistreated you. He understands he's done something wrong and is talking to you about it. Which of these two statements would you rather hear him say?

> *Guilt:* "I am such a horrible person for what I did to you. I keep doing it over and over again, even though I know better. But I just can't seem to stop. What is wrong with me?"
>
> *Remorse:* "I'm so sorry for what I did to you. This must

have really hurt you. Can you tell me more about it? I don't want to ever do this to you again."

Do the word count here. The guilt statement has six "I" words and one "you" word. The remorse statement has four "I" words and four "you" words. The difference is in the "you" words. In a healthy remorse statement, the energy and focus centers more on the injured party than the transgressing party. It conveys comfort and empathy. In contrast, the guilt statement leaves you feeling empty because it actually has little to do with you.

If the person tends more toward guilt than remorse, know that this is not by any means a deal breaker. At least she feels bad about something! She may even see the difference when you explain it and be able to express remorse to you. Some people just aren't aware of the difference. But here's why it's important to address this: *remorse decreases the chances of the problem reoccurring. Guilt increases the likelihood of reoccurrence.* You want to create a new relational path, and that requires both a change of heart and a change of behavior. Remorse is a transformational emotion. It helps a person see the gravity of what he did to a person he cares about.

Remorse is also one of the most significant change agents we experience in our relationship with God. The Bible refers to it as godly sorrow: "Godly sorrow brings repentance that leads to salvation and leaves no regret, but worldly sorrow brings death" (2 Corinthians 7:10). Guilt without remorse simply punishes a person for his or her behavior. There is no transformational experience in the relationship. The offender remains alone, beating himself up with his own club. That's why guilt never heals a character problem, a relationship, an addiction, or a soul.

Changed Behavior

Confession, ownership, and remorse provide powerful evidence of transformation in the other person. If these changes are authentic, the person naturally begins to act differently. It just makes sense that you are more inclined to change when you recognize what you have done and feel bad about it. If these three factors are in short supply, you run the risk of someone changing because they don't want to get caught or don't want your nagging or want you to stay with them. That external, compliant, and often grudging change is never permanent. It is merely a Band-Aid on a deeper problem, and you have no assurance you can trust the person's behavior.

So it's best to look for and expect changed behavior. Even with confession, ownership, and remorse, it sometimes doesn't happen. For example, he may become distracted by a problem at work or another relationship. She doesn't know how to change, so she doesn't. Or he doesn't have the resources to change right now. Still, you need to keep the expectation of change in the relationship.

As you look for evidence of changed behavior, there are three things to keep in mind: change in targeted behaviors, change in behaviors that drive more change, and sustained change.

Change in targeted behaviors. Targeted behaviors are specific actions that must begin or cease. That is, to demonstrate change, the person must start doing a good thing that is missing or end a harmful thing that is present. A desirable good behavior might be to take the initiative to connect, to tell the truth, and to be dependable. Discontinuing a harmful behavior might be ceasing to use contemptuous language, no longer acting out sexually, or quitting a drug habit. A change of heart must be accompanied by a change of action. If the person is fuzzy about what needs to change, take responsibility and spell out what you need. And be specific:

- I need for you to see a financial counselor in the next two weeks.

- I need for you to be early and overprepared for every meeting in the next thirty days.

- I need for you to never yell at me again.

Vague statements—*be nicer, get your act together, change your attitude*—will not get you where you want to go.

Change in behaviors that drive more change. There are times when an individual may not be able to immediately change his behavior. And it could be that it's not a matter of choice; something deeper is driving her behavior. In other words, the problem behavior may actually be a symptom of a deeper issue. Addiction is one example. On her own, an addict may not be able to stop taking the substance she is using, but she is still capable of other behaviors that might help. She can pray and ask God for guidance. She can attend a church that helps people with addictions. She can attend a twelve-step group. She can see a therapist and attend a support group.

In the same way, if the person in your life shows signs of being serious about stopping the behaviors that damage the relationship and *her own commitment and willpower are not working*, give her the grace and help her to find the resources that will help her change. This doesn't mean you have to tolerate abuse, addictions, or lying. These are still zero-tolerance issues. Keep your protective boundaries: the more severe the behavior, the stricter the limits. Don't put yourself at risk because the person, though truly remorseful, is not getting help. No one is helped that way. When it's a matter of *can't* rather than *won't*, go to the mat for someone who truly wants to change.

Sustained change. If you have experienced tough times with a person, you want the problem behavior to change over time — we hope forever. Pretty much anyone can change a behavior in the short term. It's called being on good behavior, and we all learned that at school — get the behavior under control and get out of trouble. But if you're going to make yourself vulnerable to someone, you need to know that the change will be sustained for days, which lead to weeks, months, and years. Then you can gradually trust again.

Be patient with the process, with the person, and with yourself. Let time pass before you open up fully again and become vulnerable. When you allow the process of growth and change to take root inside, both of you can observe what is going on. The Bible says, "Do not be hasty in the laying on of hands" (1 Timothy 5:22), which alludes to the wisdom of being careful when you make a commitment to another person. Allow some time to pass. Tell the person that sustained change over time is important to you. Observe her behavior during the different seasons of life: when she is under stress; when the two of you disagree; when he is with his family; when she is tired; when you are under stress. This is part of the due diligence of determining if a person has truly changed.

I saw a good example of this in a family I am close to. The adult son had a problem with overspending and depended on his parents to bail him out. They were constantly helping him with rent, gas, and entertainment money. He worked and had income, but he didn't work a lot — and he spent as if he worked a great deal! He had lots of excuses, all of which were very thin. His parents felt torn between their desire to care for him and the reality that they were enabling his behavior. At a loss about what they should do next, they asked for my help. So we all met together.

After hearing everyone's perspective, I told the adult son, "I am recommending your parents stop paying anything for you in thirty days. You have until then to get your lifestyle in order. I know this will be an adjustment for you. But I want you to recognize that you have hurt them, both in terms of their own financial resources and your expectation that they take responsibility for you. That's no way to treat people who have given so much to you."

I thought he might blow up at me, but instead he took the adult role and said, "OK. It's time for me to do this. I've known this all along. I don't think I could face how disappointed they were in me. They are almost as disappointed in me as I am in myself."

I was touched by his honesty and vulnerability. So were his parents. We set the plan in motion. The hard part came a few months later when his parents had to watch him move to a more modest apartment and give up his car. But they held on. And he refrained from asking them for money. His behavior truly changed over time. His parents know they can trust him now, and for good reason. Having seen how he operated in hard times, I would trust him myself.

You don't just want to see improvement. You want to see transformation. It is an entirely new way of living and choosing. Confession, ownership, remorse, and change are elements that you can use to learn to trust someone again.

The Two-Way Street

Reestablishing trust is a two-way street—it requires give and take from both people. Acknowledge your part in the relational breakdown by making sure that you too are engaged in confession, ownership, remorse, and change. Avoid the "good-guy-bad-guy" dynamic. It is a slippery slope into judgmentalism, a victim mentality, and pride. Even if your contributions to the relational problems are less severe, *do the work*. Work just as hard on yourself as you want her to work on herself. The person who commits the misdemeanor must take this just as seriously as the person who commits the felony.

The need for authentic transformation goes deeper than a problematic relationship. It's about how we conduct our lives and all of our relationships. The elements necessary for change are God's rules for health and success in life. Even if you and this person don't work things out for some reason, you are healthier, more whole, and more capable of future healthy relationships if you honor these things and apply them to your own life.

MOVING INTO THE RELATIONSHIP

Every relationship has three components: Me, You, and We. If you have worked through the Me issues in part 2 and the You issues in part 3 and feel you have the green light to move ahead in the relationship, you're ready to engage the We principles in part 4. These principles require that both of you buy into the idea that you are going to begin moving beyond protective boundaries into a deeper and more vulnerable attachment.

These are guidelines that apply to any relationship — a spouse, a dating relationship, family member, friend, or colleague. Ease in. There should be no rush here. You've done too much work for things to go off the rails at this point. But, as the process works, you should find that both of you experience what you have wanted all along: a connection that is safe, that lasts, and that helps you both become better people.

18

The Talk You Must Have

"We need to talk."

What's the first thing that comes to mind when you hear these words? A vacation? A promotion? A time of affirmation? No, never. This sentence conveys a problem, almost always a relationship problem.

The talk…

Someone thinks you have been selfish or you haven't committed or contributed to the relationship, or the school has called you about your child's conduct. If you are on the receiving end of this statement, chances are you will experience some dread and anxiety. You scramble either to avoid the conversation or to get it over quickly. Someone else is going to tell you where you're wrong and what they think you need to do about it. That creates alienation in and of itself. It comes across as parental and controlling. We tend to resist and dig in our heels in order to brace ourselves against whatever might come next.

If you are the person who says this sentence, stop it and

don't ever say it again. In fact, don't ever use the phrase, "You need to …" with another person either. Instead, say "I need …" Stating what you need is accurate and humble. Even the phrase "We need …" deflects the focus from your own need and functions as an anti-vulnerability statement. But "I" statements erect no barrier preventing the other person from being able to receive what you are saying.

"I need to talk" is the best thing to say. Even so, it still brings out anxiety in others. Regardless, you must go to the person and initiate the talk. If you want to move beyond self-protection, you must bring up your relationship and your desires and suggest some ground rules. I don't mean this as a first-date plan. The timing is when you know you are ready (based on the chapters in part 2), when the other person is ready (based on the chapters in part 3), and when you know the relationship is ready to take the next step.

Here is a rule of thumb for knowing if the relationship itself is ready for the talk: you have taken some risks over time, and the person has been warm and open with you in response. You might have admitted that you don't have a perfect life, acknowledged present and past struggles, or named some of your own insecurities and weaknesses. It's important to go slowly with these disclosures and not get too descriptive too quickly. You're just seeing how the other person responds.

If the person steps back, is uncomfortable, or shows that problems and struggles aren't something he can deal with, it may or may not indicate he's the wrong person for you. You may simply have been too disclosing for the stage the relationship is in. The talk is a way to see whether the other person's level of interest matches your own and to be clear on how the two of you can enjoy the relationship, open up to each other, and understand any difficulties.

How to Have the Talk

The talk has several aspects to it that create a structure and an agenda. You are the one who is taking the initiative, because you want to make sure things are as clear as possible between you. As you go over these, think about your own individual situation and fit it into the structure.

State What You Value and Desire

The first part of the talk is to be direct and vulnerable about the fact that the person is important to you. You value him. She is important to you. This is an essential first step for every kind of relationship—romantic, family, friend, or colleague. You would not be having a talk if the person didn't matter to you. When you affirm what you value in the relationship, you communicate that the relationship is significant, and you want the two of you to discuss it. Here are some examples of value statements:

- I care about you and this relationship.
- I appreciate the talent you bring to our company.
- You are important to me.
- Even though things have been rough, I am for us.
- You are a good friend to me.
- You matter to me a great deal.
- I still have feelings for you, even though our history has been difficult.
- I love you.
- I value your contributions to our organizations, and I like you as a friend as well.

- You are special to me.
- I'm in love with you.

Statements of value, especially of a vulnerable nature such as these, help clarify the relationship. They bring into the light what you may be sure about within yourself, but the other person may not know. Then you both know what you feel, and the other person gets a chance to respond with clarity as well. Put your cards on the table first; don't begin by asking the other person to describe the state of the relationship. That is withholding and controlling. Take the initiative and the risk. You are the one who is reading this book, who wants to pursue things with the other person, and who is learning how to move beyond boundaries.

Then ask the other person for a response. *What do you think? Is this where you are as well?* If the other person resonates with your interest, you can move ahead. But suppose you misread the signals along the way. The other person is doing an internal backflip while listening to you, didn't realize you felt the way you do, and doesn't feel ready to go deeper with the relationship. If that is the case, deal with it. It may be a brief and difficult talk, but you sure want to have it—for your own safety, and to protect the time and energy investment you make in the relationship.

But supposing the other person is interested and engaged, then what? The next step is to make a desire statement, to say what you want in the relationship. While value is about where you are now in your feelings for the person, desire is about the future. It has to do with the path ahead and what you would like to see. It may even be that you aren't looking at any major shift, such as marriage or building a partnership. It may simply be that you want things to deepen between you because you see a lot of potential. Here are some examples of desire statements:

- I'd like to spend more time together.
- I'd like to meet on some kind of a regular basis.
- I'd like us to give it a go again.
- I'd like to get to know you better.
- I'd like for us to become more open and vulnerable with each other.
- I'd like to try the relationship again and reconcile our differences.
- I'd like to date you exclusively.

Stating your desire constitutes a further and harder step into risk. It's more difficult than making a value statement because, most of the time, you can discern that there is some simpatico between you, and you are not totally on a different wavelength. But most people are much less sure about what might happen when what they want is on the table. At the same time, the other person probably knows you aren't meeting to end the relationship, so all this is unlikely to be a total shock. But you really can't predict someone's response, and the other person is always free to say he or she doesn't want to move ahead. If that is all that comes from the talk, you have still accomplished something good. The reality of the other person's response tells you for certain where things are and aren't.

But supposing you get a green light ... then what?

State Your Concern

The talk isn't all wine and roses; it needs to acknowledge the thorns. You do this when you state your concerns about the relationship. Your concern about vulnerability and trust —because of previous relational wounds—must become part of the new relationship or the new season in an ongoing relationship. This is where you apply the brakes to the connection and let the other person know, from your own viewpoint, what has happened, the impact it had on you, and what you would like to avoid this time around.

State what has happened in the past and acknowledge your part in it. You had a close relationship and trusted that you and the other person could be very open to each other. But something went wrong, and you had to withdraw from that sort of openness and establish some protective boundaries. Here are some examples of these kinds of statements:

- I had a past relationship in which trust was betrayed. I allowed things to happen that I shouldn't have.

- My ex-boyfriend had some control issues, and I didn't say no when I should have.

- The communication problems I had with you in the company were serious ones.

- I come from a family that is pretty detached and cold. They are nice people, but I didn't break out of that style and try to become more relational.

- I had a good friend who was a confidant, and she turned on me. I ignored the warning signs and didn't pay attention to reality.

- Part of our relationship has been dealing with your self-centeredness. For my part, I want to acknowledge that I have been selfish and angry with you as well.

- When you were living with your mother and me, your drug use scared us. We went back and forth between enabling you and judging you.

- There was abuse in my previous marriage. I was so dependent that I kept putting up with it.

These statements acknowledge your history and background. Stating them establishes the facts about your relational history; it is not about describing yourself in a victim or blaming role. Nor are you saying that these struggles are the present person's problem or burden. They are yours. You take responsibility for your role and contribution to the difficulties. The idea here is that you adopt an adult stance in the conversation: *I want you to know my relational past, because I don't want it to be an obstacle to you and me.*

State what you don't want to happen in the future. This is the core of your concern. You want to take risks with this person. You have worked on you, and you have observed the other person. You feel reasonably sure it's a manageable risk, not a dangerous one. With that said, you want both of you to ease into the connection, having some amount of caution. It's a little like the first jog after recovering from a leg injury. After rest and rehab, the physical therapist deems you ready to go again. As you take that first step—not a walking step, but the running kind, where you put full weight and force on the leg—you can't help but be a little hesitant at first. You don't fully relax until you've gone far enough without a shooting pain that you know you're okay. The same dynamic is true in your relationship; you need to be careful to know you're okay. Here are some examples of what you might say:

- I don't want to get hurt at that level again; it's not good for me or us.

- I want to do this right, wherever it leads. I don't want any regrets.

- I don't want to have the same kinds of conflicts with you in the organization that we have had.

- I don't want to be surprised by some new information I should have known earlier.

- I don't want to take a risk if you don't think we're close to wanting the same things for the relationship.

- I don't want to open up to you if your old dysfunctional patterns are going to return.

- I don't want to set myself up by ignoring some reality that I should be seeing.

These sorts of statements are admissions of vulnerability. You are saying that the relationship is important enough to you, that you could really be hurt if it develops and things go wrong down the line. That's openness. But it's also a warning. It's an alert to the other person—really, both of you—that this isn't a spontaneous and carefree exercise in exploring a new possibility. Though you want to have a great time and take chances, the reality is that you are going to use some discretion and discernment. You are willing to risk, but you will be thinking about what's going on at the same time.

At this point, suggest a few ground rules. They will help you both continue the exploration of the relationship and will put you both on the same page as to how to conduct this.

Establish the Ground Rules

Relational ground rules are simply basic agreements between you that help keep the relationship as healthy as possible. They provide a way for both of you to monitor the process of getting closer. All relationships need ground rules of some sort. They may be spoken or unspoken, but they are there. For example, families may need ground rules for how to have dinnertime conversation: be interested in the other person, don't interrupt, and talk about what really matters, for example. Marriages may need ground rules for having arguments, such as be there for each other, say what you want and don't want, and listen to the other person's point of view.

For a new relationship to have the most potential for helping you to move beyond boundaries, I suggest keeping the ground rules simple and few. Both people agree to the following:

- *Talk about "us."* We will make it a habit to discuss how the relationship is doing; we will do this on some sort of a regular basis, not just occasionally or randomly.

- *Be open and honest.* We will make honesty and vulnerability a normal part of the relationship rather than something we avoid.

- *Ask questions.* We are both free to ask and answer questions. If something is going on about which one of us needs clarification, we won't interpret questions as a lack of trust.

These are ground rules anyone can do. If someone is uncomfortable with these, you need to dig further. Keep the conversation about ground rules direct and then move on. Guys especially sometimes fear that a woman will want to do nothing but process feelings and the relationship 24/7, when they themselves just want a good meal and to go jogging. Make sure you clarify that you don't expect the relationship to be all about processing the relationship. You want a full relationship, which includes lots of things besides "us" talks:

fun, work, relaxing, a social life, hobbies, a spiritual life, exercise, the entire thing.

In most relationships, maintaining the commitments of your ground rules should take up a minor part of the time and energy that you spend together. In fact, the conversations themselves may be as short as ten minutes—or they could go for several hours. Whatever the length of the conversation, you need the ground rules. *In the midst of all the good you are looking forward to, you want to experience increasing connection in a safe context.* You don't want a reinjury in the same spot inside. That is unacceptable. So all you are really saying is that you are in the game and playing full court, but you want to pay attention to an old issue as you get to know each other.

Ask for Buy In

Ask for buy in: "Are you okay with all this?" This is another act of vulnerability. Having the talk and establishing ground rules isn't a matter of simply opening up, telling a person your past, and then leaving it there with, "I just wanted you to know." You are going beyond that. You are presenting your desires, but the other person has every right to say they don't share your desires—they don't want to discuss these matters, they don't have the same level of interest, or they are uncomfortable with the state of the relationship.

Suppose the person doesn't buy into the ground rules? What does that say about the relationship? Is it time to move on? No, it's not. I am not one to have a knee-jerk reaction, give up, and move on. That kind of response is how we might respond to pain or discomfort rather than a response to a person's unwillingness to buy into our ground rules. And it is not how God is with us when we don't buy into his ground rules: "He is patient with you, not wanting anyone to perish, but everyone to come to repentance" (2 Peter 3:9).

Be patient. Have a great time in the relationship. It may be that the person will, at some point, want to have the sort of relationship you've described. Remember that there are some high-quality people whose experience with deeper relational issues or with overcoming relational struggles may be limited. They may feel that they are in a world they don't know. The worlds they know are normal family life with soccer and barbeques, business and career, date night, church, theology, service, and hobbies. They may have been spared a significant relational problem or family-of-origin issue. But I have found that, even if a person doesn't have that in his repertoire, something inside him will either move toward you or away from you, and that is the important part.

An executive in my coaching program was like that. He had no experience in talking about emotional and relational matters. It wasn't his fault; he just didn't have a frame of reference for these kinds of interactions. When the people on his team revealed personal and vulnerable concerns, he likened his response to being "a deer in the headlights"—his lack of familiarity with the rules of engagement left him feeling frozen by fear. But he jumped in. He knew he had things to say and feel and face, and he moved toward the deeper relational levels. He bought in, and on the way he discovered some emotional issues that had kept him from being more open.

My encouragement to you is to not move too quickly with the other person, but not too tentatively either. Don't force it. Give yourself, the relationship, and the other person time and space for things to develop and deepen.

The talk is important. Take responsibility for determining

when it's a good time. If you and the other person are in the right place, you will most likely be pleasantly surprised at the response. We all need connection, and we all need ground rules. When you have had the talk, you are ready to live out and experience the relationship at the levels of trust that work for both of you.

19

Take a Risk

I was working with a couple who were trying to connect on a healthier level. Luis and Carmen had been married over fifteen years, and the marriage was stable. But they wanted more, especially as they saw the empty-nest years approaching. As we worked together, it became apparent to me that Luis felt insecure as a provider. They had a traditional marriage, in which he was the main breadwinner, though Carmen worked as well. But he took on the role of making sure the family was financially secure. As a manager in a retail business, he had a good income and was a competent person. However, Carmen had come from a wealthy family and had had to adjust to a different scale of living. They had never had vulnerable talks about this dynamic in the marriage. The furthest they had gone was when they occasionally encouraged each other that this discrepancy didn't really matter, because they had so many other good things going for them.

But in our time together, Luis frequently made off-the-cuff statements such as, "I work as hard as I can; I hope that's enough," and "I know it hasn't been easy for her to adjust." These statements always seemed to come out of the blue. When there doesn't appear to be a logical context for statements like these, it is often a sign that something emotionally significant is at work that must be paid attention to.

I asked him, "Do you want to tell her how insecure you feel as a provider and how afraid you are that she is disappointed in your financial status?"

He diverted for a bit at first: "It's not that bad. She has been so supportive. I think everything's fine."

But I persisted. "Luis, tell her what you're afraid of."

Finally, Luis turned to Carmen and said, "I guess I do feel like I'm not doing well enough and that you're disappointed in me."

Obviously, this was a risk for him. Both of them were positive-oriented people and tended to be a little careful with each other, not wanting to hurt each other's feelings. So this was not easy for Luis to say. I watched Carmen think about her answer. Then she said, "It has been hard. I love what we have built, but it has been an adjustment from how I grew up. But I want you to know that I am so proud of how you have provided, and I have no disappointment in you at all. I wouldn't give up what we have for anything."

Luis was relieved, but he wanted to make sure of things: "That really helps. But I don't know how to take it when you talk about how hard it is that we struggle financially sometimes. Is that about me?"

"It's about me," she said, "It really is. It's my adjustment. I'm a little spoiled, quite frankly. But I want to do better about that. I know how hard you work and how good you are at what you do. If you hear me complain, it's never about you."

The change on Luis's face was undeniable. And Carmen's

response was all he needed to feel better about his career achievements. The result was that this conversation propelled them into other substantive explorations of how they felt about themselves and each other. It was a turning point for their level of closeness with each other. Their experience illustrates how helpful it can be to bring up a concern in a relationship and how the risk itself is an accelerant into intimacy.

Doing Risk

Relationally speaking, you are now in a stretch mode, a get-out-of-the-comfort-zone mode. You want to move away from the protective guardedness that you needed at one time, and the relationship into which you're entering can help you learn to trust and live more openly again. Taking risks is a necessary part of this. But the risks you take at this point aren't major risks. This is not the time to share your most vulnerable, scary experience or thought with the person. The relationship—and the two of you individually—is being tested to see if it becomes better as you become more of who you are. You are dipping your toe, or maybe your whole foot, in the pool; but this is not yet the time to dive in head- and heart-first. It is a time to try something new, however, to see what happens.

Here is an approach to guide you through a risk with the person. It is measured, and it will help you assess the possibilities in the relationship.

The goal of risk and vulnerability in your new relationship. Taking risks and moving toward vulnerability does not mean that you immediately tell the person every detail about what you have experienced. Sometimes people are under the impression that if they don't rehash every gory detail, they are not being truly honest or that they are withholding themselves. That is not necessarily true.

Risk is not healing, and healing is not risk. Keep these two things separate. If you have been hurt in a relationship, you will probably need healing. But that will come in some other place and in some other conversations. These may be with God, a friend, a small group, or a counselor. They may involve the details of what happened so you can piece things together. But don't make this talk a healing talk. Take the pressure off both of you. The purpose is simply to deepen the connection, not fix anyone.

I recently had a conversation on a plane with a woman named Heather. She was in a career transition and also struggling in some key relationships: family, boyfriend, and parents. None of her relationships was working well, and she was experiencing a great deal of isolation, loneliness, stress, and loss. As Heather unpacked her life, it became clear that as soon as her career issues were stabilized, she needed to get some help and find a supportive community of some sort.

Noting that there were some significant trust issues with her mom that affected her current relationships, Heather asked, "If I get around some healthy people, will that solve the Mom issue?"

"It will help," I said, "but probably not resolve it. The type of trust problems you have mentioned typically require specialized treatment from an expert. Think of it this way: you need some surgery to fix the trust wound, and then you need to have a lifestyle that supports your good health."

That is the balance you need to establish in your relationship as well. Friends and lovers are for intimacy and growth. Counseling is for repair. There is always overlap, but keep them distinct in their purposes.

What the first risk might be. The first risk you take should be more about the present than the past. That is, it needs to be one of those "in the moment" risks that have to do with you and the other person—a problem, an event, or a pattern you are concerned about that the other person can readily understand and identify with, something you both know goes on between the two of you and perhaps has even happened in the recent past. While that is not always the case, it is more natural to simply peel back the onion one layer at a time as you go through life with that person. Here are some examples:

- I got scared after we talked that you would distance yourself from me.
- When I saw all the guys looking at you at the party, I got a little insecure.
- I actually didn't have a good day at work. It was pretty crummy; sorry to be a downer tonight.
- When you started giving me advice instead of listening, I began feeling alone, and I withdrew a bit.
- I really messed up in our conversation last night; I made it more about me than about us.
- I felt sad about the years we have lost in our troubles with each other, and I want better for us.
- When you were quiet, I started wondering if you were shutting down and shutting me out.
- I missed you this week and thought about you a lot.
- When you got angry and critical over the kids, it pushed me away as it did in the bad old days.

In order to make these kinds of statements, you have to be

self-aware and paying attention to your thoughts and feelings. But this is how people grow closer. I assure you, if your relationship is anywhere near normal, there will be ample opportunity to have something to say. This may not be something you do daily, but most people who are going deeper make this kind of conversation a regular part of the relationship. A few times a week is not too much, as long as there are real things to open up about and both people are into the process.

Be natural when you bring this sort of thing up. You want vulnerability to be an integrated part of the whole of your relationship. If it's appropriate in the moment, sooner is better. If you are alone at dinner, that's good. If you're at a party or watching a movie with friends, probably not. But just bring it up in the way I describe it in the examples earlier. You are developing a part of the relationship, a skill set of deeper language with each other. Don't put quotation marks on the event and say, "Now I want to be vulnerable with you." That takes it out of the "regular part of the relationship" category and can seem like a forced psychobabble exercise.

Ask for a response. A vulnerable statement generally needs a response. It's no fun to be twisting in the wind after you have taken a relational risk. You generally need some expression of empathy, interest, assurance, or understanding. The response should convey that you are okay, that the person is on your side and is not moving away, and that the risk was worth it.

If the person has the experience and skill set to provide what you need, that is an advantage. But it's not always the case. Some people talk about themselves, hoping to identify with you. Some don't say anything, paralyzed with anxiety that they'll do something wrong, and then you'll be disappointed. Some provide advice and wisdom when you want them to just assure you that they understand you. Some change the subject because it's uncomfortable. Some try to cheer you up instead of listening. So you may have to train your friends a bit, to take responsibility for getting the response you need. Here are some good examples of what it means to respond to a vulnerable statement:

- I know you were afraid I might pull away from you, but the opposite happened. After we talked, I felt a lot better about us and closer to you.

- I'm flattered that you thought other guys noticed me, but you don't have to worry about us.

- I'm sorry you had a crummy day. Tell me about it; what happened?

- I'm sorry for giving advice rather than listening; I'm still struggling with my habit of doing that. I don't want you to feel alone with me.

- When you made the conversation all about you, it wasn't fun. But it helps that you recognized it without me saying anything. That means a lot.

- You have good reason to feel sad about all the time we've lost. I've been a large part of that, and I also want to make it a new day for us.

- No, I wasn't shutting down. I was just being quiet and thinking about what you said. But let me know whenever you aren't sure.

- I missed you too. You're really becoming important to me.

- I'm sorry I was angry and critical. Thanks for telling me how it impacted you. I really want to change this behavior. I know it hurt you, and I'm taking lots of steps to turn it around.

Look at what you are constructing. You are creating a good and healthy set of conversations. They do not have to be long or complicated. You are getting to what is important so that you both can have a language for going further and experiences you both can relate to.

Wrapping It Up

Let's see what all of this talk has done for you and where it will take the two of you. Here is a summary of what I hope can occur between the two of you:

1. You have an emotional experience within the relationship.
2. You become vulnerable and let the person know about it.
3. The person responds in a warm way.
4. The relationship becomes closer and deeper.

These four occurrences can happen over and over again between you. If all goes well, you are on the way to moving beyond boundaries.

If it were possible to take risks and be vulnerable—to go beyond boundaries—by learning some principles and memorizing them, we would have done it by now. But that is never enough. Head must be followed by heart. If anyone could have successfully pulled off being a "head person," it would have been the apostle Paul, a highly educated man. Yet, in prison, he reached out to his friends and referred to how he had internalized his relationship with them: "It is right for me to feel this way about all of you, since I have you in my heart" (Philippians 1:7).

That is the process. The better the response to the risks,

the more safety. The more safety, the easier it is to peel off the next layer of the onion. And it works in relationships that are brand new or ones that have been around for decades. One couple who had been married thirty years told me, "We sat up all night talking to each other at a level we never had before." With all integrity, I can tell you, it works—and I believe it can work for you.

20

Deal with Speed Bumps

Dan and Chloe are like many couples I've counseled over the years who struggle with issues of communication and dependency. They were doing well as they learned about their relationship, but Dan was also a bit of an overachiever. He did everything to the max. When it became clear that he had not been listening to Chloe's vulnerability, he was serious about changing. He understood that he tended to dismiss her feelings as weakness and oversensitivity. For example, when she'd say that she had a hard day at work and with the kids, he'd typically say something like, "Yes, but it ended well, and you are a great mom and a great person."

Dan thought he was hitting a home run because he was trying to be positive, but I told him he was missing the point. "You need to take her experiences seriously," I said, "even if they aren't your feelings and even if you don't agree with what's going on. It's called *validation*. When you affirm Chloe's experiences, you validate them—you communicate that they're important to you."

In one of our subsequent sessions, Chloe mentioned an evening she and Dan had spent with his parents. "It's not a huge thing," she said, "but you sort of left me and spent the whole time talking to your parents about your work and what was going on in your career."

I asked Dan about his response. To his credit, he wasn't defensive, nor did he dismiss her experiences and say she was being oversensitive. Instead, he said, "I can't believe I did that again. You must have been devastated! I'm so sorry!" He went a little overboard, but that was better than underboard at this point.

Chloe went a little blank, so I picked up the conversation. "You're working really hard on hearing her," I said. "But this was just a glitch; you didn't ruin her."

Chloe affirmed this when she said, "Hey, that's okay; it's in the right direction. Thanks." And that was all that was needed to clear things up.

The couple's communication glitch was a speed bump. It was part of the learning curve of moving beyond boundaries, and it is *always* to be expected. Vulnerability, trust, and risk will make matters messy, and you will not always do this right. What follows are some things to understand, so the speed bumps don't become major hurdles for your relationship.

Perspective

Keep the right perspective in your relationship by taking the long view. If the person just doesn't get you or understand what you need to hear or what behavior you need to have, don't sweat it. It's a snag and not a derailment.

Love and relationships have to enter a learning curve as

people go deeper with each other. Allow a generous space for you two to learn how to understand each other. Sometimes an individual who has encountered trust problems will, without being aware of it, expect the other person to read her mind. So when she says X and the other person's response is not the response she needed, she will feel unloved and disconnected. It is as if the relationship is a dartboard, and the other person is expected to hit the bull's eye. Not even the greatest psychologist in the world can hit the bull's eye every time.

This dynamic usually has to do with a long-standing pattern of not being understood by others over many years. The individual begins to retreat from relationship and reverts to an old childhood desire that someone understand her without her having to explain herself, in the same way a good parent understands a child's facial expressions, tones, and body language on a deep intuitive level. She often does this because she is resistant to taking a risk and believes at some level, *If he loves me, he will figure out what I am feeling without me having to say what I need.*

A trained therapist can help with this dynamic, but it's unrealistic to put this expectation on someone in your real-time life. So forget the bull's eye. Look for care, interest, and effort. They will pay off for you. And understand what it's like from the other person's perspective. You probably would like to have some direction and help from the other person about what he needs so you don't spend endless hours trying to create the magic empathic words that make him feel appreciated.

When someone doesn't seem to understand you but is making an effort, technically speaking, that is an empathic failure. But an empathic failure is not an emotional injury. It can trigger one and remind you of it, but it's a communication problem, not a psychological wound. It helps to keep that in perspective. If you find that the other person's fumbling around does impact you at a deeper level and you can't shake it, it's probably a sign that you need an expert to help you with this so you can take the pressure off both you and the other person.

Remember, however, if you are experiencing serious problems—which suggests the person has some character issues, addictions, or deceptive tendencies—this is a different matter. It's not a speed bump. It could be harmful to you and jeopardize the relationship. If that happens, you must address it and confront it. Tell the person what happened and that you are concerned and things must change. Keep your protective boundaries in place. You may even need to tell the person that for things to go further, you need to know that he or she is getting help from a professional source. Guarding your heart, even while you are working on becoming more open, is a lifetime task.

The Most Common Speed Bumps

The more informed you are about speed bumps, the more able you will be to deal with them successfully. There are some typical kinds that, once you understand them, will cover most of the obstacles you will encounter. Here are some of the things that can happen between you and the other person and what you can do about them.

Miscommunication

The other person doesn't understand what's going on with you, and the vulnerability-response cycle doesn't go well.

There is no bad guy here. In fact, don't even say anything about it; just say what you are saying in a different way that might be clearer to the other person. Take responsibility for how you are communicating. For example, "No, the problem wasn't that I hadn't prepared for the presentation. I was just scared that I would make a fool of myself." Then ask, "Does that make sense?" Restating things in a new way often enables the person to respond with more understanding. If communication is a failure time after time, you may need to get some help on that. Harville Hendrix's book *Getting the Love You Want* has a lot of good skills ideas for this problem.[11]

Innocent Triggering

Sometimes a person accidentally says or does something that triggers an old hurt from the past. If it is a new relationship, the reaction can be from your previous connection, your family of origin, or both. If it is a current relationship that you are trying to rebuild, it may be something that person said or did that echoes the unhealthy way you related in the past.

For example, a friend of mine was dating a very nice woman, and I liked seeing them together; I thought they might be a good fit. However, his previous girlfriend had been highly critical of just about everything about him—his clothes, his friends, his habits, and his speech. It was not a good situation. He barely survived that relationship. The new girlfriend was not that way at all. But when she made a direct statement that was appropriate, he become defensive and felt attacked by her. If she said, "I didn't like the movie," and it was a movie he had picked, he felt the comment was an accusation of failure.

In situations like these, it's as if one person is a minefield. When the other person innocently walks across a buried wound, the minefield person explodes in fear, withdrawal, or anger. If this happens and you are the one who is triggered, don't make the other person the problem. Tell her your defensiveness or withdrawal is about your own baggage, and you're committed to working on it. Ask for patience with this issue that you both want to resolve.

If it is the other person who is triggered, do not react. Don't explode or get defensive. Be there for him, listen, question, understand, and empathize: "So when I said I didn't like the movie, did it feel as if I was putting you down? That is so far from what I was thinking." Most of the time, the person who was triggered can then see that it was not about the two of you and can move on.

Learning Curve

Skills for mature relationships are learned over time. Even people with great relational experiences and abilities have to learn the particulars of the other person. This is the interesting part of getting to know someone, as we are complex and unique individuals, a trait for which we praise God: "I praise you because I am fearfully and wonderfully made; your works are wonderful, I know that full well" (Psalm 139:14).

Suppose, for example, that your idea of a way to unwind after coming home from a dinner out with friends is to sit with your spouse and talk about what you noticed and experienced at dinner. But your spouse's idea of unwinding might be to chill out in front of the TV, browse the Web, or take a walk to clear his or her head a bit. That difference isn't about you; it's just personal preferences. It is about two people with different styles learning to adapt to a relationship.

Character Issues

Character issues are often more serious than speed bumps. If they are severe enough, they can jeopardize the relationship. A character issue can be transformed if the person is honest about it, demonstrates a desire to change, and is getting help from some resource besides you. If those things are in evidence, you can reasonably expect that there will be personal growth and change that will eventually enable love and vulnerability to happen.

An executive I know almost blew his marriage out of the water with a character issue he didn't want to face. He was financially irresponsible to the point that he and his family almost lost their home. His wife was frightened. When she was vulnerable about her fears, he became angry and blamed her for the money problem, saying that if she were more supportive, he would do better financially. I pointed out that while he might have a point about her lack of support, she was not perfect. But I said that her lack of support was no excuse for his financial problems. At that point, he blamed me for siding with her, and it was a mess for a while.

This is a painful illustration of how character is the most serious of the obstacles. If you see it, nip it in the bud, and don't drop the subject just to keep the peace. Character issues never get better when they are ignored.

Having gone through some of the most common things that can go wrong, here are some guidelines that can make a difference when you encounter a speed bump.

Skills to Help You Get Over the Speed Bumps

There are a few basic competencies you can learn that will go a long way to resolving the speed bumps. If you and this person will be together a long time, you will also be able to use these in the future whenever disconnections arise. They will help you recalibrate the relationship.

Talk about Talking

People who want to improve a relationship often talk about talking. That is, they bring up what happened and what went wrong in their experience and come up with solutions. Here are some examples:

- Remember when I said I need space and listening, not solutions and homework assignments? It happened again; let's fix this.

- I don't want to sound childish, but I've been trying to be more open about the job problem, and it still feels as if you want just good news from me about work. I really need you to hang in there with me.

- It feels as if you're impatient with me when I go to a deeper level now, as if I ought to have my act together. That's hard for me; are you really feeling that way?

- When I brought up the problems I have with my dad, you lost eye contact and started talking about something else. This is really important for me; are you okay with all this? Is there a way I can do this differently, or do you not want me to talk about this with you?

Be a team player with the person. In responding, you must have no hint of judgment or a critical spirit. You are forging a way to connect, and never forget that the "we" comes first. You want to recruit the person to vulnerable language, to solve the glitch and move on.

Acknowledge that maybe you aren't being clear or that this is new for both of you. Vulnerability works both ways. If the other person feels a lot of performance pressure to "get it right," she won't be able to speak from her heart. And you are after a heart-to-heart attachment; that's the whole idea. I have coached many husbands on how to be empathic. Lots of them don't naturally know the right things to say, so I give them some examples that I hope trigger and resonate with what they really feel toward their wives. Statements like these are good examples:

- That must have been hard.
- Tell me more.
- How did that make you feel?
- That's tough; anything I can do to help?

These are simple things to say that convey understanding and support. Guys being guys, they often say, "Great idea," and write them down so they can remember them. The problem comes when they run through the list and recite them! Most wives catch on in about three seconds, and then there is a talk about the talk about the talk. So let the person know, "You don't have to do this right; I certainly don't myself. I just need to know you feel something positive toward me when I am feeling negative." And that covers many errors.

Banish Shame

If you're both trying to open up and go to a deeper level, be generous in extending grace, undeserved favor. Be for each other, for the sake of the connection. Don't have a talk every time the person doesn't get it. That can lead to discouragement and feelings of failure. And keep it positive, shame free. When sex therapists help their clients, one of the things they do is to banish shame in the bedroom. A couple needs to be able to bring up questions, observations (not mean ones), thoughts, and desires without the internal judge ruling things.

Love can't rule when shame is in charge. The same is true with vulnerability. There are many parallels between emotional vulnerability and sexual intimacy, because of the vulnerability of being naked in one sense or another. Adam and Eve had that experience in the beginning: "Adam and his wife were both naked, and they felt no shame" (Genesis 2:25). Exposing your heart should be welcomed in the relationship. If you can both laugh about your mistakes with each other, at least the ones that are not damaging, you go a long way toward banishing shame.

Persevere

Things won't always feel close, and there will be disconnects, but don't give up too quickly. Be willing to persevere — even if you don't feel close or hopeful. Get back on the horse again. Great relationships that last a long time always have some periods in which the individuals feel alienated from each other but decide to face each other again and work out the problem. Perseverance means doing the right relational things — like the principles in this book — even when there is no real passion behind it. It's sticking to God's deep values of love, grace, honesty, ownership, and stewardship.

Perseverance is about working through trends and patterns, not simply with events. Anyone can be occasionally flaky, in a bad mood, or impatient. These are isolated events in the relationships, not the whole picture: "A person's wisdom yields patience; it is to one's glory to overlook an offense" (Proverbs 19:11). Overlook the wrong. Look for the trends and patterns. Is the flakiness, moodiness, or impatience coming up regularly when you try to connect? Are you seeing a series of events that are similar in nature? Are objective people in your life observing the same thing? If so, that's different. Even so, as I've mentioned, it may not be time to end things at all, just time to take the patterns more seriously.

But even perseverance has its limits. You can't persevere just by trying harder over and over again. There are always two things to consider when you persevere in working through vulnerability speed bumps as you seek to move beyond your protective boundaries:

1. *Be energized from the outside.* If things aren't working well, you must not do this alone. It is not possible to continue taking risks when you are in isolation from everyone but the person you are trying to connect with. Make sure you are getting encouragement and support from others.

2. *Change what needs to be changed.* If you are continually experiencing withdrawal, blame, irresponsibility, or deception on the other end of the relationship, it's no character virtue to keep taking risks that aren't working. It's been said that insanity is doing the same thing over and over again and expecting a different result. That's a problem.

So give the person, yourself, and the relationship lots of time and room to make mistakes in vulnerability. As you continue to deal with the obstacles to intimacy, they will be less discouraging over time, and you will simply experience them as a normal part of relational life. Work through the small stuff and put your energy into the larger issues.

21

How Far Can You Go?

"If you don't want to settle in your relational life, this book is for you."

Those are the words that began this book. Everyone has experienced some form of pain, disappointment, and discomfort in a significant relationship. Most people have had to set up protective boundaries and withdraw from trusting in order to prevent bad things from happening again. But you don't have to settle for a life of isolation, guardedness, or polite-but-distant relationships. As I hope you have discovered as you worked through the issues in this book, your relational life can move beyond boundaries into intimacy and deep friendships, if you take the right steps.

However, you have to ask the question to yourself: What is the potential here? Can we continually grow deeper? How far can a relationship go?

What's the Potential?

I believe that with two willing people, the potential for intimacy in any relationship—be it romance, family, or friendship—is almost unlimited, bound only by the constraints of time and energy. Intimacy is a part of love, and we are designed to continue growing in love: "From him the whole body, joined and held together by every supporting ligament, grows and builds itself up in love, as each part does its work" (Ephesians 4:16). We interact with each other in love in an ongoing process. The work of intimacy is continuous and increases in growth over time.

There is no reason to assume that at some point, you have reached relational nirvana with the other person, and you both can coast from there. We are complex beings, and there is always something to discover. My parents have been married more than sixty years. They can often finish each other's sentences. *And often they cannot.* My father will surprise my mother with an opinion or an observation. My mother will do the same. There is no sense of hitting some bottom level of intimacy in which there is absolutely nothing left to discover about the other person. My father told me recently, "I am still fascinated by your mother." And it is true. Whenever our family visits, we see the engagement they have with each other. It is a good model for all of us.

But intimacy was never reserved for marriage alone. The love that the Bible teaches is not the exclusive property of married couples. If you are single, you have the same potential in your own relationships for a gradual deepening of knowing and being known by others. You need a few people around you with whom you can take the risks we've discussed in these chapters. Pursuing intimacy can be part of your lifelong growth process as well.

I met recently with a friend of mine who has been single for many years. She likes her life. She is open to marriage but isn't doing anything to pursue it these days. I asked her about her relationships. She has lots of friends, but there are several she considers family. Some of them are biological, literal family, and some are not. She has been close to them for a long time. Her experience is that they are all still getting to know each other. She sees no end in sight in the increasing depth of vulnerability in these relationships, nor do I.

Explore These Aspects of Each Other

Where does increased intimacy lead and in what directions? Fortunately, there are many paths to explore. You are designed to know and be known. Don't go through life with someone and miss out on being intentional about noticing the following aspects of the other person. There is a lot you can learn if you pay attention, whether it be over coffee, at a party, or working out at the gym. The context is not as important as what you are seeing in each other.

Your Emotions

You both have feelings. Some are positive, such as happiness, joy, and a sense of accomplishment. Some are negative, like anxiety, fear, guilt, and sadness. There are many emotions and combinations of emotions. They lend texture to the relationship and help connect you to each other's hearts. Do you know what makes each other happy? Sad? Mad? Why is this so?

Your Values

Values are realities that are important to both of you. Some values are the same for both of you; ideally, the foundational ones, such as God, love, honesty, and freedom. Shared foundational values are essential because they provide a bridge of connection between the two of you. That's especially important because there will be other values that are not the same. However, that's not a negative, just a difference. These ways in which you differ provide an opportunity to see each other and life from a different viewpoint—and to grow as a result. Each of you should sit down and list your core personal values. What are the similarities, and where do they differ? Are the differences important; are they topics for further discussion?

Your Character

Discovering more about how each of you is hardwired inside has great potential for shared vulnerability and interest. Your capacities to enter into relationship, to be empathic, to be direct, to take ownership, and to deal with problems are critical to your own life and the way the relationship develops. Write down what you think are each other's character strengths, without the other person seeing them. Compare notes. Are there any surprises between what you two perceive in each other, and the way you see yourselves?

Your Competencies

Everyone is good at something: sports, music, literature, computers, finance. Help each other discover and develop these strengths. There is always room to grow and achieve. Identify each other's competencies and tell the other person how those competencies make your life better in some way.

Your Losses and Injuries

There are experiences that have been painful for all of us. Mistakes, hurts, even deaths of significant people. Make sure you know, understand, and can talk about these experiences with each other. There are far too many relationships in which these are avoided, and that limits the potential of your connection. Tell each other how knowing the other's losses moves you toward one another.

Your Preferences

You like and dislike different things. These are not moral issues or better versus worse. They are merely stylistic. One of you likes parties, and the other prefers a quiet dinner. One of you is linear, and the other is creative. One of you wants a high-church experience, and the other wants something more edgy. Understanding preferences helps you appreciate the other person's individuality. List several preferences you have, some of which are similar and some of which are not. How do you handle the differences and still stay connected to each other?

Your Past

You both come from somewhere, and your background helped form who you are, for better and for worse. The more you understand each other's early lives, family dynamics, culture, and religious life, the more you know the present person. What are a few of the most important realities about your past that affect the relationship you are crafting with each other? What family dynamics are the most important? Do these realities cause a problem or a benefit?

Your Future

Everyone has dreams and passions for the future. Some may be looking toward a financial dream; some a career; some a location; and some a way to serve and give back. Get to know each other's dreams for the future. Set out your dreams: mine, yours, and ours. How do they intersect with each other?

Your Relationships

You know a person by knowing her friends. She picked them for a reason. Her friendships reflect a great deal about her, and they also continue molding the person she is now. They can be a source of great connection for both of you. What can you learn about each other as you understand the friends? How do you relate to the other person's best friends?

Your Quirks

We are all a little weird, fearfully and wonderfully made. The eccentricities shouldn't be a matter of distancing but of connection, even fondness. One of you can't walk out of the house without the dishes being in the washer. One of you can't walk past a pet store without going in. What quirks do you notice in each other, and how do they affect you?

You Two

We've been over "the talk." But never forget to continue the talk. Keep checking in on the relationship and asking periodically, "How are we doing?" "How do we affect each other?" It is something Barbi and I do in our marriage. It is also something I do with my closest friends. I'd rather have a checkup than have to undergo relational surgery.

As you can see, there are many ways to get to know another person and to allow him or her to know you. Getting to know another person never ends; it is a process and a journey to be enjoyed.

The Elements

In addition to what makes you up as people, there are a few necessary elements for this ongoing and permanent process of continued and increasing openness. They are ways to approach the relationship and to improve the quality of what you have with each other. If both of you possess these, the relationship can have great potential. Make these elements part of how you relate to each other.

View Closeness as a Means and an End

Both of you want to connect not only for the benefits, but also because you care about the other person. It is not that you are open because it's a medicine that you have to take to stay healthy. Closeness has pleasure and joy inherent in it. We should feel good after a meaningful connection, unless it has been about some sort of pain or problem. Some people have found that connection is difficult, mainly because of negative experiences with a past relationship. That may be true initially, but once vulnerability begins to happen, that should resolve in time.

Establish a Structure for Connection

Intimacy is somewhat organic and natural, but you also need to focus on it. People who like each other tend to spend more and better time together; you naturally want to be with someone and to be open to someone with whom things go well. But life can take over. We all have lots of demands that take our focus: work, other relationships, family requirements, and finances, to name a few. To avoid losing relational ground, it's a good idea to have some sort of a structure that helps you both carve out the quality time that a great relationship needs. Don't depend on your attachment and connection and say, "We'll talk soon." Reserve that for relationships that aren't so vital.

I always suggest both a logistic and an intention in establishing a structure. The logistic is to set aside time to be together without distractions. It's just the two of you for some amount of time. The intention is that you agree you'll both open up and go deep. It will be more than a catch-up on the events of the day or week. It will be how you both are doing, in the areas noted above. It's probably best for one person to be the initiator of this. My experience is that one person is more hesitant about going first, and you don't want to spend all that time waiting for relationship to happen spontaneously.

Build on Depth

Use risks and vulnerability to continue the process. As you become safer and more assured that you both are truly for one another, you will be able to risk increasing levels of honesty. This is simply how closeness goes. You were made to be known, and when you know the conditions are right, you move toward that. And your own vulnerability will attract the same in the other person: "Deep calls to deep" (Psalm 42:7).

Commit Yourself to Spiritual and Personal Growth

If both of you are involved in spiritual and personal growth, most of these other elements will fall into place. The growth process of following God and his path, of relating authentically to others, and of dealing with your own issues will be a source of continued intimacy for your relationship.

The two of you are not enough for each other. You do not possess all of the sources of energy and motivation for what you need. That is not enough, and it will limit both of you. You need to be in a continuing course of God's growth, help, encouragement, change, and transformation. You need to be following him and his Word, deepening yourselves spiritually and relationally, following a path of growth, and being in a healthy church environment. Then you and your relationship are constantly being refreshed and reenergized.

Take the pressure off the relationship to provide all you both need, and be people who are reaching out for growth. There is no reason that you can't be in some sort of a growth process for the rest of your life, from a small-group environment, to friends who are growing, to a vital spiritual life.

The only real limitation to intimacy is the investment each of you makes. It takes two people. Some individuals will get to a certain level of closeness that is suitable for them, at least for the time being. They view additional growth as too much work, not important, or uncomfortable. If that is the situation, you cannot do the work for them. It doesn't mean the relationship is over, by any means.

Some of this depends on context. If this is a relationship you are committed to, such as a marriage or with a family member, then adjust and adapt to the other person's limit. Find out if you are part of the problem and are somehow pushing the other person away. Help them with any concerns or fears they have about openness. Beyond that, don't pressure them. Love them, be a great relationship for them, and accept their freedom and choices. Put your energies into the good things in the relationship and into your other friends and activities. But make sure they know the door is always open to more closeness, should they want that.

Don't burn your bridges. I have seen situations in which a spouse or friend went through a personal crisis, a business loss, or a spiritual epiphany and all of a sudden, they were looking for more in a relationship. Don't live in a deprived state, but stay open to change.

You do not have to settle. God did not settle when he created you and when he established relationships with you and him, and with you and people. Your connections, and possibly the one you are working on as you read this book, can be something that will bring you fulfillment and growth for a lifetime.

Beyond Boundaries into Your Best Life

I hope you are now encouraged and more equipped to move beyond relational struggles from the past so that you may enter a deeper and more vulnerable connection with those who matter most to you. You will always need your defining boundaries, as they make us who we are and clarify us so that we can reach out to each other. But the more you can move beyond your protective boundaries in your most important relationships, the better you will experience the intimacy you were created for.

Making the effort to develop intimacy is important not only for your connections, but for your entire life. You were meant to be free, not careful; open about yourself, not closed down; capable of deep attachments, not disconnected. You were designed to follow love and live in love, becoming like the One who embodies love itself: "And so we know and rely on the love God has for us. God is love. Whoever lives in love lives in God, and God in them" (1 John 4:16).

The work is worth it. May you find the life that God intended for you in the journey.

God bless you.

Dr. John Townsend
Newport Beach, California, 2011

Notes

1. Henry Cloud and John Townsend, *Boundaries: When to Say Yes, When to Say No, to Take Control of Your Life* (Grand Rapids: Zondervan, 1992).
2. Neurobiological research is now presenting evidence that trust may even be affected by brain chemicals. Researchers have found a connection between oxytocin, sometimes called the "cuddle hormone," and trusting relationships. When they artificially increased the amount of oxytocin in people, those individuals actually trusted others more than they normally would. The emotion of trust and how we process relationships is affected by our biology. Regardless of how the research will trend, trust is an aspect of life that is central to all our relationships (Paul J. Zak, "The Neurobiology of Trust," *Scientific American* [June 2008], 88–95).
3. S. L. Murray, J. G. Holmes, and D. W. Griffin, "The Benefits of Positive Illusions: Idealization and the Construction of Satisfaction in Close Relationships," *Journal of Personality and Social Psychology* (1996), 70, 79–98.
4. I describe sadness more extensively in *Leadership beyond Reason* (Nashville: Nelson, 2008), pp. 71–77.
5. Henry Cloud and I write more extensively about the need for relationships in *How People Grow*, chapter 7, "God's Plan A: People" (Grand Rapids: Zondervan, 2001).
6. Rick Warren, *The Purpose Driven Life* (Grand Rapids: Zondervan, 2002).
7. For additional guidance on how to pay attention to your emotions, see my book *Leadership beyond Reason* (Nashville: Nelson, 2008), chapter 8: "Emotions."

8. Henry Cloud and John Townsend, *Safe People* (Grand Rapids: Zondervan, 1995).

9. I always ask this question when the person being discussed is not present. Otherwise, there is the risk of distortions and perceptions —not reality—being the issue.

10. See my book *Loving People* for additional guidance on how to develop the skills to connect at that deeper level. *Loving People* (Nashville: Nelson, 2007), chap. 3: "Connecting."

11. Harville Hendrix. *Getting the Love You Want* (New York: St. Martin's Griffin, 2007).

Embark on a Life-Changing Journey of Personal and Spiritual Growth

Dr. Henry Cloud   Dr. John Townsend

Dr. Henry Cloud and Dr. John Townsend have been bringing hope and healing to millions for over two decades. They have helped people everywhere discover solutions to life's most difficult personal and relational challenges. Their material provides solid, practical answers and offers guidance in the areas of *parenting, singles issues, personal growth,* and *leadership.*

Bring either Dr. Cloud or Dr. Townsend to your church or organization.

They are available for:
- Seminars on a wide variety of topics
- Training for small group leaders
- Conferences
- Educational events
- Consulting with your organization

Other opportunities to experience Dr. Cloud and Dr. Townsend:
- Ultimate Leadership workshops—held in Southern California throughout the year
- Small group curriculum
- Seminars via Satellite
- Solutions Audio Club—Solutions is a weekly recorded presentation

For other resources, and for dates of seminars and workshops by Dr. Cloud and Dr. Townsend, visit: **www.cloudtownsend.com**

For other information **Call (800) 676-HOPE (4673)**

Or write to:
Cloud-Townsend Resources
18092 Sky Park South, Suite A
Irvine, CA 92614